Travels with the Doggie Lama

An unsettling near-crime. An impulse purchase. Two events conspire to unite a struggling twenty-something with an errant, adventure-loving companion. Join two divergent spirits on their journey through joy, sorrows, and finding their way through life.

By Lily Tanzer

Copyright © 2018 by Doggie Lama Books, LLC, a subsidiary of Causal, Inc.

All rights reserved. This book or any portion thereof may not be reproduced or used in any manner whatsoever without the express written permission of the publisher except for the use of brief quotations in a book review.

Printed in the United States of America.

First Printing, 2018

ISBN 978-1-62747-205-0
eISBN 978-1-62747-207-4

www.DoggieLamaBooks.com

Dedication

To my husband --
home is wherever you are

To my parents --
you both taught me from an early age
that faith is a miraculous force

"There is a magnet in your heart that will attract true friends. That magnet is unselfishness, thinking of others first; when you learn to live for others, they will live for you."
— Paramahansa Yogananda

"True friends always bring donuts."
— The Doggie Lama

Foreword

This book is all about love.

Keisha, a roaming bundle of love on four legs, is sure to capture your heart and put a smile on your face from the very first page of this wonderful tale. You will fall in love with her colorful antics and mischievous personality—just as I did, and continue to be!

And when you're finished reading, I guarantee that you will wish you could pick her up in your arms and carry her home with you.

And while *Travels with the Doggie Lama* is a rollicking, fun-filled adventure, it isn't a cute pet story. Far from it. It is a powerful saga about the loving and life-changing bond between two kindred spirits—a remarkable dog and a distressed woman who found a best friend when she needed one most. It is also a moving and poignant reminder that, when our spirit is open, the Universe will fill our heart with unconditional love in ways we never imagined possible!

Ironically, the genesis of this unique friendship was a deeply disturbing incident, an emotionally shattering attempted break-in that left Lily feeling victimized and unsafe. She wanted a protector to restore her sense of security and ward off any future crime against her. Enter little Keisha—two pounds of pure kinetic puppy love gift-wrapped in a soft package of shiny dark fur. From the start, Keisha was irrepressible—born with a renegade soul, an irresistible charm and a knowing gleam in her eyes. As she grew older it became increasingly apparent that Keisha's destiny was to be more of a spirit guide than a guard dog. And the special connection that quickly formed between Keisha and Lily soon enriched both their lives. Through Lily, Keisha found a loving home and devoted master; through Keisha, Lily managed to transform her fear into a sense of adventure and a desire to fully embrace life.

It doesn't matter if you are a life-long dog lover, or someone who has never had a pet; this story will touch your heart because it speaks of the transcendent power of love to bring true joy into our lives—whether we happened to be born with two legs or four.

I was blessed with the opportunity to meet Lily through a Vedic palmistry consultation. Her handprints revealed a square below her index finger (the Jupiter finger), which is a sign of wisdom that carries the signature of a natural writer. I remember remarking to Lily during our first consultation that she should try her hand at writing a book. I am so glad that she did, because *Travels with the Doggie Lama* is a gift to the world, a beautifully crafted gem that both entertains and inspires! The language sparkles with Lily's genuine humor, which effortlessly conveys pearls of wisdom and spiritual insights—a reflection of Lily's wonderfully idealist heart line!

Both Lily and I share a love for the teachings of the great spiritual leader, Paramahansa Yogananda, as well as a passion for the meditation and spiritual awareness Paramahansa encouraged us all to pursue. That passion shines forth throughout the book you are now holding in your hands; it is a passion that is certain to strengthen your faith in yourself and in your connection to Spirit. To develop deep, unshakable roots in any relationship, our love must be supported by a strong spiritual foundation. The story of Lily and Keisha brilliantly illustrates how we can lay that foundation with warmth, kindness, compassion and, most of all, unconditional love.

Thank you, Keisha and Lily, for sharing that love with us, and for giving the world this beautiful love story!

>Guylaine Vallée
>Certified Vedic Astro-Palmist
>Author of: The Happy Palmist:
>My Adventure in Vedic Palmistry

Chapter 1

I awoke with a start.
Rolling over and blinking to clear my eyes, I managed to make out the glowing red numbers.

2:34 a.m. I always loved it when the numbers marched in sequence.

Then the sound that startled me awake repeated itself.

It took a moment to make sense of the noise; my sleep had been deep and I was disoriented. My apartment, in the middle of a big city, was usually filled with a constant stream of urban hum but something was out of place and had awakened me.

The noise was coming from my front door.

My breath seemed labored and too loud as I strained to make out the noise. Someone was prying at the lock and jiggling the doorknob.

I could sense, in some odd way, the intent from the other side of the door and it felt strange, malevolent perhaps. My heart pounded and I tried to catch my breath. So this was it: what my mother had warned me about living alone in a big city. "YOUNG WOMAN VICTIM OF VIOLENT CRIME", the headline would read in the papers.

As the adrenaline flooded my body for a quick escape, time seemed to be altered into snapshots.

The front door: the only way out. But that's where the sound was coming from. The windows.

They were narrow crank-style windows original to the old apartment, but the drop was two-stories to a concrete sidewalk. Maybe. If I could shimmy through, a broken leg was the probable outcome.

My little apartment, cozy and warm earlier that night as I fell asleep, was now my prison.

The sound at the door seemed deafening in the still silence of the night. I crept from my bed toward the kitchen. I saw the phone; if I called for help the intruder would hear me, as I was only a few feet from the door. That might be good. Or not. He may flee or he might ratchet up his attempt to get in. Did he just want my possessions or did he have more sinister intentions?

My heart pounded in my ears and my mind raced. In the darkness I tiptoed to the kitchen, trying not to make a sound. I needed something to defend myself.

My mind and my eyes struggled to focus.

More snapshots: a steak knife in the sink. I grabbed it. A skillet on the stove. The adrenaline in my body made it seem light as a feather. I stood in the kitchen, staring at the front door, the only thing that protected me from whatever evil force waited on the other side.

The summer night was warm but as I stood shivering in my nightgown, the knife in my right hand, the skillet in my left, thoughts came fast and furious, meeting the tempo of my heartbeat.

I could picture the faceless intruder lunging towards me; he'd have to be within inches of me before my weapons would be effective. But even then, would I be physically strong enough? Self-preservation and the need for survival flooded my body; a primal force was taking control.

The sound at the door had stopped, but my heart pounded in my ears. I continued to listen, vigilant for any movement outside the door.

Nothing.

I was finding it hard to breathe.

I waited for a few seconds. I crept cautiously to the door, praying the old wood floor would not squeak and betray me. Standing as still as I could, I listened, my breathing and my heartbeat deafening. But I could hear nothing coming from the door. I waited a few more minutes and still nothing. My body began to relax a bit, my breathing less labored. Maybe they had gone and I would be safe.

I moved cautiously toward the phone. I picked up my lifeline and dialed the number of my landlord who lived across the driveway. The phone trilled. I peered through the window to his apartment, dark and silent in the next building. With one ear monitoring the ringing, my other ear strained for any other sounds coming from my front door. I disconnected the call and dialed the closest friend I had, Anna, who lived only a couple of miles away. Thank God she was close.

I waited anxiously as the phone shrilled in the receiver. At last she picked up, groggy with sleep. In short bursts of breath, I managed to bring her up to date and soon she was knocking on my door, the most welcome sound I had heard in a long time.

I wanted to see physical proof of my would-be assailant. We stood at the small landing outside my door, which I shared with apartment #4 just a few feet away. That apartment had been vacant for months but seemed extra quiet in the dark night air. Its emptiness may have been the only witness to the scene we were now investigating.

A cigarette butt was next to the door mat of my unit. No one in my tiny complex smoked. This was out of place. Someone had climbed the stairs that led to my apartment and stood at my door. I didn't imagine it. Someone had been there.

For anyone who has experienced a violent crime or natural disaster, the loss of security and safety tampers with the implicit contract life tends to hold. Danger lurks around every corner. While no real official crime had happened to me that night, my world had shifted on its axis as if it had. Whether or not my would-be intruder had intended to steal my belongings, they had stolen my sense of safety.

I quickly packed some essentials in a bag and headed to Anna's apartment where, for the next week, I camped on her old, stained couch. Chandon, Anna's regal champagne-colored Chow-Chow, at first was not particularly happy with my presence. The couch, positioned in front of a large picture window, provided the perfect look-out to view all the comings and goings in the courtyard of the apartment complex. And my presence was a clear impediment to his sentry position. But after a couple of days, I liked to think he had accepted me as a new fixture. I was also another member of the apartment to guard and keep safe.

That first night, after packing my belongings and heading to Anna's apartment to try and catch a few hours' sleep before heading to work, I lay on her couch, staring at the ceiling. Chandon lay across the room staring at me. His head resembled a lion; his thick, blond mane ringed his face and his dark eyes quietly watched me in the half-light of the room. My luggage sat near the couch, hastily packed. The room was quiet in the early morning hours. I could see the calendar posted on the wall near the kitchen, and my eyes traveled to the date: September 8, 1988. That day is the moment where my world felt unsafe, where I had felt the presence of something strange beyond my front door and my internal sense of equilibrium had careened off center.

    I had narrowly escaped meeting the mysterious person on the other side of my front door. A meeting that may have ended fatefully. Yet little did I know that escaping the encounter would lead me to meet an important player in my destiny, to alter the course of my life. And my heart.

Chapter 2

"Really important meetings are planned by the souls long before the bodies see each other"
— Paulo Coelho
Eleven Minutes

The waiter poured steaming coffee into my cup. That first sip never failed to lift my spirits and the oily, astringent taste signaled the coming wave of caffeine that would soon have me seeing the world in a more optimistic, or at least more focused, view. It was nice to savor the rich brew in its gleaming mug rather than the hasty cup that I downed each weekday morning to jump-start the day. Sunday brunch was, in my opinion, one of the highlights of the week. Anna and I sat at a corner table of a café in the arts district, bustling with the clatter of silverware and the noisy buzz of the diners. The starched white tablecloth and miniature vase of fresh flowers certainly added a few dollars to the price, but after the week I had endured, over-priced-but-aesthetically-pleasing was a necessity, not an indulgence. The eggs benedict were laden with enough butter to hold me until this evening, so

I was still being economical, as I wouldn't need food for hours.

We had grabbed the Houston Chronicle, another jewel of Sunday mornings, with the intent purpose of looking through the ads for dogs. I had decided a good watchdog was the answer to my now shaky sense of safety. Chandon convinced me that Chow Chows were the gold standard in personal protection; they were known to fiercely guard their masters, instructed by the DNA of their Chinese ancestors and prized for their aggressive, protective nature.

"Pass me the classifieds" I said, after we had placed our order. We were going to skip the weddings section and our ritual "Rate the Bride" game today (being in our mid-twenties, most of our friends were dropping like flies to the institution of matrimony) and get to the business at hand.

"How much do you think Chows cost?"

"Several hundred, I'm sure," Anna replied. "They definitely aren't cheap."

Another kink in my budgetary constraints, but as always I soldiered on.

I scanned the column for the "C"s and found that Anna was right. AKC registered Chows were indeed several hundred dollars. Where was I going to get the money to buy what I had decided I absolutely needed? The ads were looking progressively bleak when my eyes caught this simple entry:

Chow puppies $75.00
(713) 555-5742

My heart rate was already elevated from the coffee and now took off in a full sprint. My dream companion, my earthly protector, was perhaps waiting at the other end of that telephone number. And totally within my price range. Ancient Chinese personal protection, all at a discount!

We finished up the budget-busting brunch and headed back to my apartment to call the owners of the puppies. The woman on the other end of the phone explained that only one puppy was left. Runt of the litter? Oh no, she explained. This little girl was the pick of the litter and had been earmarked for a family member who had, at the last minute, decided they didn't want a dog after all. Serendipity or a bait-and-switch sales technique? Who knew?

Anxious to not miss out on the last pup, we agreed to meet at 3 o'clock and I was given the address.

Anna and I went to her apartment to check on Chandon and then headed out to meet my potential partner. The afternoon was warm and the sun had the heavy golden light that comes in the fall and infuses the leaves with the rich colors of autumn. We headed out Highway 59 and left the city behind us. The houses became sparse as we drove through the sprawl of suburbia and finally arrived in the country. A series of turns on single-lane roads led us to the opening in wooden post fencing, which we entered to find the one-story ranch house so typical in Texas. The oak trees spread their gnarled branches across the lawn, offering shade to the green grass below. The sun was still intense despite the fall weather. A middle-aged woman clad in pink slacks and a white cotton Oxford shirt met us on the sidewalk and introduced herself as Maggie. She guided us around the house to the backyard.

The yard was flat and well-manicured, surrounded by the same wooden fencing as in the front, enclosing the acre or so that surrounded the house. Another wooden fence housed a couple horses further back from the house, lazily munching on grass. The three of us were quiet; there were few sounds except for the pebbles crunching beneath our feet and the occasional whinny of a horse. A strange kind of anxiety gripped me—a mixture of test driving a new car or meeting a friend's third cousin for a blind date. We finally arrived at our destination—a small cardboard box at the far end of the concrete patio. We approached the box and peered over the side to see a small, black dog nestled against a tattered towel in the corner. Maggie scooped up the squirming ball of fur and held her up by the scruff.

"Here she is!" she announced.

The pup flailed her tiny paws as if swimming in the air. Her black eyes peered nervously at me and Anna. Spending so much time with Chandon's imposing bulk and imagining my own intrepid guard dog, I was caught off guard by the diminutive butterball staring back at me.

"Here," Maggie said as she thrust the dog into my chest. Reflexively, I cradled the pup, but with the trepidation of holding a newborn baby for the first time. My awkwardness was met with an equal amount of distrust on the puppy's part. She became very still as she tried to assess the situation.

"Pick of the litter," Maggie proclaimed. "My sister and her three boys were going to take her but at the last minute decided they weren't ready for that kind of commitment. She's eight weeks old and already had her first round of shots." Maggie seemed impressed with the last bit of medical news. It meant very little to me, but I nodded as if to acknowledge this accomplishment.

My grip on the dog softened as I became more comfortable holding her. She, in turn, seemed to relax a little and sought refuge against my chest. Her fur was downy soft and black as coal. As were her eyes. Her ears were tipped at the ends and her short muzzle was framed by a shock of fur on both sides. Her coloring could be described as jet-black except for a few strategic spots. Each paw sported a wisp of white at the tips, and a blaze of white fur traveled up the center of her chest and stopped abruptly at her throat. She resembled a baby bear.

"The ad said she is a Chow?" I asked, not taking my eyes off the little dog and needing to realign my vision of Protector Extraordinaire with this plump baby.

"Her mom is a pure-bred black Chow. The father is a Husky from next door." She nodded her head toward the property behind me. "He managed to jump the fence and get to our dog," she explained, allowing only the tiniest disapproval at the illicit coupling to cross her face.

The $75 price tag now made sense.

I managed to shift the pup to one arm so that I could hold her face. I pried her little jowls open to look at what should be, I thought, the tell-tale black tongue of the chow. Her bright pink tongue wiggled and lapped at my fingers.

"So no black tongue, then," I said to Maggie.

"No," she said, flatly.

The puppy continued kissing my fingers and I noticed a small black dot off to one side of her tongue. Aha! A small but important mark-of-the-Chow had managed to find its way through the mixed genes and express in this tiny little mark. The royal lineage had been besmirched by the rogue next door, but a telltale sign had managed to emerge.

"So half-Chow, half-Husky. She'll be a pretty large dog, no?" I was still holding onto the image of the stocky Chandon.

"I would estimate around 60 pounds or so," she confirmed. Hard to believe the wiggling two-pounder I was holding would someday be such a sturdy animal.

I looked around for evidence of the mom and dad but saw nothing.

Maggie stood quietly watching us.

Not one for impulse purchases but faced with going home empty-handed to an apartment where I still didn't feel safe, my mind raced with trying to reconcile the bargain-priced, pink-tongued puppy with the image of my warrior pure-bred Chow. As I wrestled with my racing thoughts, Anna grabbed the puppy and cooed into her tiny muzzle.

Maggie didn't seem to be one for the hard-sell. She remained quiet while I grappled between my desires and the reality of my bank account—a perpetual battle that had plagued me all too often. I had imagined a trip to Bloomingdale's to pick out a new Louis Vuitton handbag and instead found myself in the back alley, fingering a knock-off that resembled the real-deal but failed any test of authenticity.

Anna, still holding the bundle of fur, had been smitten and urged the reluctant shopper to close the deal and run.

"She's adorable. We'll stop at the pet store on the way home and pick up her supplies."

Oh good, I thought, more purchases.

I pulled out my checkbook and confirmed that Maggie would take a personal check. As she nodded, I thought how unaware Maggie was of the danger of that decision. My personal checks tended to be their own kind of Russian roulette.

Before I knew it, we were back in my car with the cardboard box and my new roommate. Anna seemed delighted with my purchase but I felt more than a little unsure as to what had actually transpired. Somewhere in the daze of driving back to the city, a name had been decided upon. It was all a muddle. The check had been written, the box and its contents had been placed in the back seat and the journey home to my now-changed life had begun. Keisha was now a part of my household and would grow, hopefully, to be the avid protector that I longed for.

We drove 45 minutes back toward the city and slowly the skyline came into view on the horizon. The setting sun cast a glow to the glass and metal buildings, reflected back from the boxy and angular giants rising from the density of the island of skyscrapers. But before the freeway curved its way around the conglomeration of architecture, we took the exit to my apartment and navigated through the streets lined with restaurants, retail shops and car dealerships. The autumn light receded as we pulled into the parking lot of a pet store. My impulse purchase had awarded me the new role of caretaker of an innocent, wiggling puppy with none of the accoutrements to carry out the mission. The parking lot was almost empty, not many shoppers on a Sunday evening, and felt a bit bereft. Not unlike me.

Sunday evenings were meant to be quiet, relaxing hours before the stress of the new week and preparations made for the coming stress of work or school. And boy did I have preparations for this week. Food, collar, chew toys, leash and goodness knew whatever other essential and probably expensive items were needed for my new life with Keisha.

Anna had been energized by the whole event and felt sure that my new life-with-a-dog was just what the doctor ordered. Keisha stay curled in the box while I followed Anna into the store as she counted off on her fingers the various items we would need.

Several hours later, the cardboard box had found a home on the floor beside my bed. Keisha sat in the center looking up at me with quizzical eyes. Her new red collar, the smallest one the pet store carried, had been knotted in the center to ensure it would not slip off her tiny head. The knot sprouted out the top of her black scruff, lending a Quasimoto-like effect. We had spent the evening playing together, although her rough-house play would end abruptly as she would collapse into my lap and take a restorative nap for 10 or 20 minutes. Frenzied play would resume after a refreshing snooze.

I now explained to her that it was 10:30 and time to go to sleep. Her head tilted to the side acknowledging that I was trying to communicate. I bent over the box and arranged the ragged towel, her parting gift from Maggie, while I continued on with my explanation of the need for a night's sleep. It occurred to me that Keisha was probably only hearing the "Wa-Wa, Wa-Wa-Wa-Wa" that represented adult's voices in the Charlie Brown cartoons. I could drone on all I liked but my little dog didn't speak English yet.

Hoping that non-verbal communication was still an effective route, I turned off the bedside lamp and tucked into the bed. Moonlight streamed in through the windows and the shadows of the leaves outside danced against the covers. I held my breath. No sound from the box.

Most nights found me in a similar pose in the darkened room, holding my breath fearing another potential intruder. My sense of safety had been seriously damaged and turning off the lights at bedtime always heralded the deep panic of that fateful night.

But now my breath was being held not for fear of my own safety but for concern over this little being taken from the only home she had known, thrust upon this anxious stranger, and now was meant to relax into her new environment here in the dark. I slowly let my breath out.

A rustle from the box.

I quietly drew a breath and held it again, careful to not make a sound and disturb the occupant of the box. I was optimistic that the quiet darkness would signal bedtime and the sleep she seemed so easily to slip into earlier.

More rustling. My hopes began to fade.

The rustling grew frantic and the squeaks began. "Eeps" would be a more precise description. I lay very still in the bed, allowing the emotion coming from the box to disperse and hopefully play itself out. I glanced at the clock: 10:33.

I'd give it 5 minutes.

But things seemed to be heating up down on the floor. Amidst the "eeps" and "peeps" the box began to move and I could make out the sound of tiny paws clawing the sides of the box.

I dared not move. Surely things would calm down. My magical thinking had theorized that the stiller I could be, the more it would calm the frenzy that was now brewing beside the bed.

Magical thinking is usually just a coping mechanism and rarely works. This time proved no different.

I glanced at the clock. The red numbers glowed 10:35.

This was Keisha's first night away from her mother. I envisioned her snuggled into the belly of the black Chow, whiffling in sleep, feeling safe and secure with the sound of her mom's heartbeat in her little ear and the familiar smell filling her nose. A wave of sadness swept through me.

I thought back to my childhood struggles of leaving my mom: watching her wave goodbye on the first day of kindergarten. Later, sleepovers where the loneliness I felt, resting in the darkness while all the other girls had drifted to sleep, was oppressing. I would lay very still and feel the heaviness in my chest, alone with thoughts of my mom who seemed so far away I doubted her existence. Nothing ever felt as safe as crawling into my mom's lap and bur-rowing my head into her chest. And hearing her heartbeat.

Perhaps we never completely disconnect from that primal need.

Wasn't there something about putting a clock in the puppy's bed? The ticking was supposed to mimic the sound of the mother's heartbeat. I mentally scanned the apartment and came up short. The digital clock radio next to my bed would offer no help.

I felt anguish at what this tiny creature must be feeling. She had seemed to cope so well with all the events of the afternoon, distracting her from the separation from her home. And now reality had come in the darkness. My feelings of security had been quashed a few weeks ago and now Keisha was experiencing the same loss. My eyes stung with tears of compassion. I looked at the clock: 10:36.

I couldn't take it anymore; I needed to console my puppy.

I flipped on the bedside lamp and light flooded the room and illuminated the scenario in the box. The white-tipped paws were clutching the frayed top of the box and a wet, black snoot was trying to work its way over the top. I leaned over the box and her dark eyes sparkled and the little tail began to swish feverishly from side to side.

It occurred to me that the deep sadness and loss of maternal comfort that I had conjured while remembering my own struggles was not necessarily what appeared looking back at me from behind the cardboard walls. The wagging had become so violent that her back paws were becoming tangled in the towel. The wet nose sniffed fiercely, trying to reach my hands. I reached into the box and scooped her up onto the bed. The furious wagging continued and the pink tongue lapped feverishly at my face and hands.

Short squeals of delight emanated from her little body.

I cradled her next to my chest and stroked her downy head. She seemed to calm down and soon had burrowed her snoot in the crook of my elbow and fell fast asleep.

I held her for a few moments and then, with the skill of a Zen Master, moved her toward the box ever so slowly, hoping she could not detect the slightest movement. Holding my breath, I watched her face for any sign of awakening as I lowered her gingerly down towards her nest in the box. The whiffled breathing continued in an easy rhythm.

My hands cradled her two pounds while my eyes searched for the perfect nest in the towel. Ever so cautiously I positioned her into the folds of the terry fabric and now began to extricate my hands from underneath her belly and rump. Continuing to monitor her face for any sign of wakening, I saw the slightest change in breathing and a flutter of her closed eyelids. I stopped and willed the molecules of air around her to freeze. After a few seconds, the breathing returned to a consistent pace and her eyes remained solidly closed. I resumed the extrication of my hands and with adroitness I did not know I had, placed her squarely on the towel. Keeping my eyes peeled on her face, I backed away from the box and reclined back onto the cool sheets. I lounged there, watching the ceiling but all other senses honed on to the box to check for any signs of movement. Only a slight snore drifted from the towel.

After a few more tense moments, I reached to the bedside stand and turned off the light. The click of the switch seemed deafening and my body stiffened. Frozen, I listened. No snores but pure quiet.

Relaxing, I leaned back against the pillows, closed my eyes and breathed a guarded sigh.

The box rustled.

A squeak.

Clamoring amidst the cardboard.

The light was turned on again, the soothing words flowed and the cuddling resumed. More lowering into the box, more consternation and howls of recrimination. After an hour or so of this drill, the white flag of surrender was raised and Keisha was allowed to snuggle among the blankets and pillows with me.

Contentment seemed to ooze from her very being and she drifted happily into sleep. My concern and empathy for her abrupt removal from her mother and everything she had known had proven to be illusion on my part. I looked down at the ball of fur, curled snoot to tail, and acknowledged that the only trauma that night had been my dogged attempts to make her sleep in the box.

She was now where she belonged.

Chapter 3

"And suddenly you know: it's time to start something new and trust the magic of beginnings."
— Meister Eckhart

A recent article in a magazine listed the top ten Life Events that create stress:

1. Death of spouse
2. Divorce
3. Marriage separation
4. Jail term
5. Death of close relative
6. Injury or illness
7. Marriage
8. Termination from job
9. Marriage reconciliation
10. Retirement

Some of the events weren't necessarily negative; they could actually be happy ones like marriage or a new job. Yet change, in and of itself, is stressful.

Nowhere on this list was "Acquisition of Puppy" but I attest that it should be somewhere between jail term and injury or illness. Once those sweet little paws cross your threshold, things are never the same.

Getting a puppy, whether it's a well-planned decision or a spur of the moment one, takes your life and flips it on its side like a sumo wrestler. You hit the floor with a THUMP, you lose your breath for a moment and you say goodbye to life as you knew it.

My life, until Keisha arrived, had its share of ups and downs: the stresses that come with relationships, forging a career, and the usual self-absorption that comes with being twenty-something. I had been an ultra-responsible child and my Type-A personality drove me to achieve with a laser-like focus. But after graduating from college, I found myself completely adrift. I had always done best with order, structure and a firm game plan. My love of list making was legendary.

Starting at about age seven, I had forged a New Year's ritual of purchasing my new calendar, chosen with great thought and discernment. The artwork or photographs of each month would set the tone for the year. I would purchase it with my Christmas money, which I had added to my little safe stored under my bed.

Having purchased the document outlining the coming 365 days, I sat at my desk and wrote the important dates on the crisp pages of my new calendar. It was deeply comforting to turn the pages of and see the grid of days laid out in such order. As I flipped through the months, I could envision the changing seasons and imagine what adventures might await me. Life was meant to be planned and directed; spontaneity had eluded me for as long as I could remember. Even my childhood imaginative-play most often included being an accountant or banker; stacking the piles of play money, neatly segregated by denomination.

My New Year's ritual had continued for many years but had waned during college. In fact I didn't even keep a calendar anymore. I had learned to store all of the details in my head, a talent that amazed many but seemed second nature to me. My brain loved to file the details in its various folders and try to make sense of the progression of time.

If I had managed to complete my calendar ritual the New Year's Eve leading into 1988, the year Keisha arrived, I wonder if I would have stopped at October's grid and in some clairvoyant way, felt an important meeting was coming.

As I had grown older, my organization skills and perpetual planning had eased and I now found myself in a new phase of life for which I had no plan. Career plans were dubious if non-existent, my love life equally bleak and at an even deeper level, I had no clear idea of who I was. I felt rudderless as if sailing through a heavy layer of fog.

So now I found myself needing to learn a new way of living. I was meant, it seemed, to learn the art of living in the moment, steering my rudder with the mercurial winds dominating this new phase of my life.

When the student is ready, the Master arrives.

Chapter 4

*"It's comforting that
even the Pope has an
overwhelming urge to quit his
job on Mondays."*
— Unknown

Life at Apartment #6 on Lake Street was about to take a sharp right turn once I carried the cardboard box from Maggie's bucolic backyard across my threshold.

While our first night ended with Keisha getting her way, eschewing the cozy nest I had created for her in the box and instead demanding my own sheets and blankets, Monday morning brought with it a whole new power struggle.

As much as I disliked Sunday evenings, Monday mornings held a unique distaste. It didn't help that I was working at a job I felt held me prisoner five days a week. Monday mornings never failed to feel oppressively grim. I was staring down five whole days of drudgery.

But this Monday morning held a new challenge. I still had to haul myself from a too-warm bed, slog through a shower and don my corporate garb. But now I had to somehow figure out what Keisha was going to do while I spent 8 hours in the salt mines.

And, I was yet to learn, contain the destruction that was possible while my little dog was left unsupervised.

Clearly I had not thought this whole dog-thing through, and for a brief moment I contemplated calling in sick so I could forge a game plan. While that thought brought an intense feeling of relief (and a spontaneous grin to my face), I soon remembered that I had several important projects waiting on my desk. Monday gloom returned and my smile disappeared.

I needed to clear my head, so I plopped Miss Keisha into her box and went to shower.

The scalding water did much to soothe my nerves but I soon became aware of a strange commotion in my bedroom. I grabbed the shower curtain and pushed my head as far as I could away from the water, turning my head back and forth like a rabid owl, trying to hear the noise.

Odd sounds like a soulful howling punctuated with.....yes.....attempts at barking. Dripping wet, I walked to the bedroom and saw the cardboard box being shaken by scratching paws. Then puppy-howls and now the ever-emerging skill of barking.

"I'm just taking a shower!" I said to the box. "YOU ARE FINE."

Back to the shower I plodded and the howls and general consternation continued. My morning shower was one of the best parts of my day and my attempts at blocking out the hubbub in the next room were proving too much for a Monday.

Exasperated, I left the steamy bathroom again to be met by the same level of commotion as before.

Leaning over the box, large plops of water dropped from my hair and shoulders onto the towel inside, with several landing on the black fuzz covering Keisha's head. I scooped her up and carried her into the bathroom, depositing her onto the middle of the white and black tile floor.

"Okay, sit here while I finish my shower," I announced.

The verbal tirade had quieted while my morning ablutions continued amidst the steam. I heard no rustlings from beyond the shower and realized I had not closed the bathroom door. Drawing back the shower curtain again, I peered across the room looking for the plump little bear. My heart quickened as I realized the room was empty except for various piles of dirty clothes. In a bit of a panic, I pulled the curtain completely open to investigate the possible destruction that could spread beyond the bathroom walls and, as my right foot cleared the top of the tub, I saw her.

She had shimmied into the corner where the tub met the wall and sat, with her back paws protruding between her front feet and her snoot pointing to the opening of the shower curtain. Her belly spilled unabashedly onto the floor. Buddha was seated. The mist and steam escaping between the wall and the shower curtain had drifted down onto her fur and sat poised, like the first snowflakes of a winter storm, atop her face, head and back. Her fur now had a mottled gray look.

She seemed unperturbed, actually content, that she was able to get as close to me as the architecture allowed. Her black eyes blinked and I noticed her lashes had a caught a few drops of moisture. I was struck by how tender her face looked and realized that no one had ever been so content to be within a foot of my presence, mist and all. But there was no time for tender moments. The clock was ticking.

Her tail swished feverishly against the white tile, but her rump remained firmly planted on the floor.

"Okay, just let me finish," I sighed. I closed the curtain as best I could but noticed, now, the steam and water droplets escaping through the break and traveling down to a waiting, satisfied puppy. I continued with my shower, knowing a pair of dark eyes rested just beyond the curtain.

Keisha seemed to revel in the rest of the preparations for work, even eagerly investigating the turquoise-blue makeup bag I hauled out each morning. She sniffed the tube of mascara and the blush compact and finally settled in to chomp on the corner of the bag.

Managing to wrestle it from her jaws, I tossed the bag onto the bedside stand and grabbed her new leash, bright red to match her collar. I clipped the lead onto her and off we headed to the grassy area below my apartment. She was too small to navigate the open stairs, so I carried her down, noticing she was still a little moist from the shower. I plopped her onto the dewy grass and encouraged her to poop and piddle. Not that she knew what that meant. But it was my understanding that this was one of the first steps in housetraining.

My high heels sank in the moist earth while I waited. She sniffed each blade of grass like a scientist exploring the cellular patterns of a newly discovered life form. The thick humidity in the air was causing my pantyhose to stick to my legs. Mosquitoes buzzed around my ankles.

I looked at my watch. I had my morning routine calculated down to seconds. I was already 10 minutes behind schedule.

"Go poop and piddle, Keisha," I encouraged, tugging at her leash to break the sniffing reverie and pulling her to a new spot. My heels sank into a fresh spot of earth and Keisha renewed her investigation of another patch of grass. A mosquito bit my shin.

Our struggle of wills seemed to be a recurring theme the last few hours. I tugged again and she hunkered down, determined to continue her olfactory interrogation of the grass. My sunglasses were now foggy from the morning humidity.

It seemed that there wasn't time to coax the desired outcome here. Housetraining would have to wait. I whisked her off the grass and carried her back up the stairs. I had already decided that the kitchen was the best option for hosting Keisha's day. It offered a fair amount of contained space and the linoleum floor could be easily cleaned. Next to the trash can I set up her water dish and a "bathroom" of newspaper from the Sunday's edition. I deposited her new rubber pork chop toy and her new ball. The towel from her box was laid next to the water bowl.

Everything in place, I was happy with the cozy environment I had fashioned.

Putting her atop her towel, I petted her back and kissed the tiny space on her forehead between her eyes. This would become our morning routine.

"Bye, Little Miss. I'll be home for lunch, if I can."

I closed the kitchen swinging doors behind me and realized there was no latch to keep them closed. I grabbed the red leash on the table and wound it round the two knobs of the doors, figure-eight wise, to secure Keisha's corral. I could see, through the slim opening between the doors, Keisha's dark eyes watching me.

I grabbed my purse and keys and headed for the front door, keeping one ear trained to the kitchen.

Quiet.

Locking the door, I headed downstairs and stopped, below the kitchen window to listen for any signs of trouble.

Oh, my, I thought. This could turn out very badly.

Yet no howls, no hubbub emanated from the small window.

I had a knot in my stomach by the time I arrived at work. I grabbed a cup of coffee from the break room, settled into my cubicle and tried to focus on my daily routine. I felt sticky from my trek in the apartment yard.

Thoughts kept drifting back to the helpless, scared, and vulnerable puppy sitting alone in my kitchen. Twenty-four hours ago I didn't even know she existed and now I couldn't concentrate on anything but this tiny animal now in my care.

I had honed my worry-abilities to the level of "Expert" through the years, often working myself into a state of sheer panic. This life-long skill now had me speeding home, taking an early lunch, to visit my new roommate and make sure she was still alive.

Practically running up the uneven stairs, I flew through the front door and turned immediately to the kitchen doors. The red leash, thankfully, was still wound around the knobs. Light coming through the crack in the doors was bright from the noon sun streaming in from the window over the sink, and shifting my eyes downward I saw a small shadow. A frantic snuffling noise emanated from the kitchen and because I was slow in opening the doors, an agitated squeal soon followed.

Released from the confines of her kitchen, Keisha's small body pounced on my feet and amidst squeals of delight, jumped and nipped at my knees, snagging my last pair of good nylons. I bent down and bundled her into my arms. Her pink tongue licked feverishly at my face and she continued her squeals, now shifted from agitated to joyful.

I managed to look past her rabid licking to the room beyond. Strewn across the linoleum were the remains of the newspaper, shredded and wet with urine. Small paw prints had tracked poop across the room and the water bowl had been overturned. Her towel had been pulled to a new location and the chew toys were nestled against the kick-plate of the cabinets.

Aromas that should not exist in a kitchen floated up through the humid air.

Someone had been busy.

And I had never felt so appreciated or wanted in my life.

As we began to know each other better, I learned that Keisha's personality was at times nuanced and other times blatantly dramatic. Her devious side, while plotting to swipe morsels of food off my plate or quietly steal away under the couch with my new $32 bra, was well concealed with only a wispy glimmer in her eyes or tell-tale twitch of her nose.

That week we settled into our daily routine, the mornings following pretty much the same path, including Keisha's sentry at the bathtub. By week's end she had begun to associate my turquoise makeup bag, the zipper now completely chewed off, with my leaving. Once she spied it in my hands, Keisha would throw her chubby little body against the ground and begin to whine and wail like a character out of the Greek tragedy, Antigone.

I noticed that life seemed to be handing me a cruel lesson of late—each time I criticized or was judgmental about someone, I found myself doing the very thing for which I was critical. And yes, I had scoffed and rolled my eyes at people who were besotted with their animal. Good heavens, I thought, it's just a DOG. Why in the world would anyone put so much energy into someone who lived for chew toys and rolling around in the mud? There were more important things going on. *Get a life*, I thought.

And here I was, once again, standing in the spotlight of my own judgment. I was obsessed with my new family member and was building my life around her needs. Calls to my phone message recorder in the middle of the day so I could tell her I was thinking of her. Planning my schedule around her schedule. In fact, I realized, I may now be the worst offender when it came to focusing my life around my dog.

I was able to come home each day for lunch and our evenings had us partnering with Anna and Chandon for walks in the steamy evening hours. Keisha, upon meeting Chandon for the first time, was clearly struck by Cupid's arrow. She flipped and somersaulted in front of him, licking his muzzle and face. She nearly quivered with love for this stately, masculine dog. Chandon stoically sat very still and, through gritted teeth, waited for Keisha's energetic ardor to calm down.

Anna's boyfriend was immersed in his studies, so their time together was often limited. I was woefully unattached, so she and I spent a lot of time together after work and on the weekends. Our friendship was deep and comfortable and the addition of our dogs into our inner circle was natural and offered a fair amount of entertainment.

Anna's short, curly dark hair and wide, blue eyes were in direct contrast to Chandon's long, blond mane and narrow dark eyes. Their personalities offered the same contrast—Anna was easygoing and laughed often, while Chandon was serious and quiet.

Keisha and I, too, were a study in opposites. My long, blonde hair and worrisome view of life seemed at odds with her short, black fur and devil-may-care approach to adventures.

We were an interesting party of four.

Chapter 5

"Hearts will never be practical until they are made unbreakable."
— The Wizard of Oz

"You've done WHAT?" my friend Jonathan yelled through the phone.

"I have a new puppy," I repeated, trying to keep the excitement that had originally been in my voice still intact.

"You know what this means, don't you?" he said in the parental tone he so often intoned.

"What?" I replied, rolling my eyes like a petulant teenager.

"Fourteen years." He took a dramatic pause. "Then Heartache City," he flatly stated, presenting my dismal future.

I was a bit confused at first.

What in the world was he talking about? What happens in fourteen years?

Jonathan had been my friend since high school and we had attended the same university. Our time in college brought us closer and we had continued our friendship after I moved to Houston and he entered law school. Now in his third and final year, his hours in mock-court had only enhanced his already theatrical and authoritative delivery.

My confusion and surprise at his statement had brought the conversation to a halt. I wasn't quite sure what to say (or do). Perhaps I should just hang up. This conversation didn't seem to be going well.

"Surely you remember Duchess," he said in the tone that television lawyers so often use when dealing with problem witnesses on the stand.

Oh, yes. Duchess. I had heard on more than one occasion about Jonathan's beloved dachshund. Duchess had been one of the happiest parts of Jonathan's childhood and dear Duchess had slipped into doggie senility during her last months. She spent her time walking aimlessly round and round the backyard pool, pausing only briefly to stare into the blue water, looking as if she were contemplating the troubling state of world events. After a decent amount of laps, she would wander into the house, up the stairs, into his mother's closet, orient herself to face the wall and then deposit her rump upon the floor. There she would sit for hours staring blankly at the wall among the hanging skirts and shoe trees.

Finally, her health had diminished even her ability to complete her daily closet duties and at the age of fourteen she had been put down. Duchess's death had been a very traumatic event for my friend.

"She lived fourteen years," he went on, not bothering for my response. "Fourteen years filled with happiness," he sighed wistfully.

Though now studying law, Jonathan had been a music major in college and had always been drawn to the arts, readily apparent in the soliloquy he was now delivering. I sensed that on the other end of the phone, his head must be turned stage left and his hand resting Hamlet-like on his chest.

"She was my best friend. Everything a boy could ask for in a dog," the prince of Denmark continued. "She was sweet and loving. I remember how we used to go for long walks along the beach in Florida. Then when we moved, she was my constant in a time of huge change."

As the thespian continued his stroll down memory lane I could picture the regal Duchess, her short legs sturdily supporting her long frame while her chest held its noble pose. I'm sure her dark eyes glistened with the wisdom and enlightenment that surely had been apparent during those magical years.

"Fourteen years," he repeated, breaking my reverie of the other-worldly Duchess. "And then...Heartache City."

We both sat silent on the phone, feeling in some shared way the still raw wound of her loss. Not liking the deep feeling of pain emanating through the receiver, I shook my head to bring common sense back to the exchange.

"Oh, Jonathan, that's ridiculous. You know what they say," I offered. "'Tis better to have loved and lost than to have never loved at all.'" I thought Tennyson might have said that.

Surely Jonathan couldn't negate all the beautiful memories of those years for the pain that came with losing her.

I heard the scoff and felt the contempt on his end.

"Yes, that's what they say isn't it?" We were back to the imperial voice of the litigator.

I continued my anemic argument in support of opening one's self to love, even if it meant possible pain and loss. I just couldn't believe that someone as young as Jonathan could be so resistant to the vulnerabilities that love often brought. Although we had been on earth the same number of years, Jonathan's voice held the cynicism of one who has lived events that rob the soul of joy. Not normally being an optimist myself, I desperately clung to my stance that love was worth the risk and I noticed that my voice had become decidedly shrill as he continued to negate my argument.

And yet I wasn't acknowledging the same wounded and now cynical part of me that had sought refuge in a different city several months ago. I pushed my own pain down into its cage. And tried to lock the door.

We ended the call without resolving our opposing beliefs, each hanging up the phone with a sanctimonious pout, sure in the knowledge that the other had been ignorantly wrong.

This was the first real negative response I had received from anyone on the news of my now being a dog owner. I had quickly dismissed my mother's standard reaction to this kind of news: "Do you know how much work it's going to be?"

Most of my mother's major life-decisions were based solely on maintenance and upkeep—would it show dirt easily and how hard was it to clean? Keisha represented a walking mine field of spills, stains, destruction and major disorder that sent shivers down my mother's spine.

But both my parents seemed oddly supportive of the new acquisition. Who can resist a cute pup?

But it did occur to me now, after hearing the sadness and pain in Jonathan's voice, that both my mother and father had similar tales of a childhood dog whose death had been more than traumatic.

I had heard so many times about Blitzi, my mother's German shepherd, and Boots, my father's collie, that I automatically tuned out the repeated stories of how much those dogs were loved and missed. My father's tale always ended with the same foreboding announcement that when Boots died "something in me died that day, too." My mother was just as melodramatic in her recounting of the pain she still felt in losing her pet. Each time they recalled the play of events, the pain seemed fresh and unbearable. Both of them, just as Jonathan had done, vowed they would never get close to another animal again. They armored themselves against any future scars. Tennyson and I both shook our heads at the cynicism of those three.

I looked at Keisha now, splayed on the floor, destructively chewing her rubber pork chop. Her ears wiggled as she gleefully gnawed the red and white plastic. How could anything so cute and innocent be cause for alarm?

And yet I recalled the flood of tears that came while watching Old Yeller's death on the television. Or trying to hold in my sobs at the movie theater when in junior high, Rose Brown, Lisa Middleton and I spent a Saturday afternoon watching "Where the Red Fern Grows."

As the death of the coonhound Little Ann played out across the movie screen and the theater became thick with shock and sadness, the three of us stiffened in pain and desperately tried to hold back our emotions. Hot, stinging tears clouded my view of the tragedy projected on the screen, while Lisa quietly reached for the sleeve of my sweater in my lap. She dabbed at her tears with the sleeve as they rolled in a flood down her cheeks.

Rose let out an embarrassing squeak in the hushed room, and I glanced in her direction but could see little through my own tears. She had always carried a few extra pounds on her stocky frame and even in her deep sorrow, managed to lean over after the merciful end of the scene and whisper to me, "I hope there is still some fried okra left when we get home." Food was always a consolation, and Mrs. Brown's famous fried okra would be needed that day.

It did seem that there was a primal anguish with the loss of something as innocent and loving as a dog. But I wasn't going to waste any time thinking too deeply about this. I had made the right decision and Keisha was proving to be so much fun. They were wrong anyway, I thought defiantly. It **IS** better to have loved and lost.

And fourteen years was a long time away, anyway.

Chapter 6

*"Why does drama
follow me wherever I go?"*
—Unknown

The $75 I paid for Keisha included her first round of shots. I later learned that puppies require a laundry list of vaccinations those first few months of life, administered on a rigid schedule. So I grabbed my checkbook and headed to the local veterinarian's office to complete the inoculations that Maggie had begun.

"What a cutie, this little one is," Dr. Beck cooed as she stroked and petted Keisha.

My little dog had immediately been wary as I hoisted her up onto the cold, metal examining table. When Dr. Beck swooped in, the alarms began to go off. Keisha's eyes widened, her body stiffened and as the examination proceeded, her legs began to flail in a desperate attempt to escape the physical interrogation. She nipped, in vain, at the doctor's probing hands. Clearly Keisha had read the Marine's survival manual that stated one's primary goal is to resist capture. And if captured, the next plan is to escape.

The examination mercifully complete, Dr. Beck, with small beads of sweat forming on her brow, stepped away to gather the last part of our visit—the shots. I tried to pacify Keisha with a calming hand and soothing words. Keisha was having none of it and proceeded to buck and kick like an angry bull in a rodeo pen.

Dr. Beck returned with three menacing looking needles, firmly grabbed Keisha's little behind and skillfully pushed the shots, one after another, into the fuzzy rump. The assault stunned my little dog and the flailing halted. Keisha's glistening black eyes turned to me in a helpless panicked request for help. My stomach churned while my heart pounded. There was nothing I could do. Keisha squealed a couple of times and continued her verbal response with a dog's squeaking version of "that REALLY, REALLY, REALLY hurt. REALLY, REALLY, REALLY. OW, OW, OW, OW."

"All done," the doctor announced. "It will stop hurting in a few seconds," she said, trying to reassure both of us.

She lifted Keisha from the table and plopped her onto the floor to allow Keisha to shake off the assault. The vet and I stood at the stainless-steel table discussing the information I now was gathering for my new life raising a puppy. Keisha continued her verbal tirade.

OUCH, OUCH, OUCH, she lamented, trotting the perimeter of the room, searching for the escape route. A Marine is tenacious in attaining the goal.

As the doctor and I continued our discussion, so did Keisha's protestations. After five minutes, the calm Dr. Beck turned to look at my complaining dog, paused for a moment and then turned back to me.

"There is NO way she still feels those shots," she said, her eyebrows furrowing, and revealing an increased level of annoyance.

My discomfort grew, the initial layer being from the kerfuffle of the exam and shots and now laden with my dog's insistence of complaining about the entire affair at a level that had begun to irritate the general public. It did appear that the lamentations were more theatrical than a genuine expression of pain.

Not wanting to prolong the increasingly annoying display, I gathered the complaining ball of fur along with the brochures and handouts that were to guide me through the successful journey of puppyhood, and headed to the nearest exit.

As I settled our account at the front desk, Keisha continued her verbal harping on the attack.

OUCH, OUCH, OUCH.

As we wound our way through the parking lot, my own nerves frayed from the ordeal, I finally snapped.

"Yes, I KNOW it was horrible. Believe me, I didn't enjoy it either. But you didn't have to write a big fat check at the end, either," I complained, referring to my now wounded pocketbook. Heaven only knew what this was going to do to the health of my already anemic bank account.

The whining stopped but Keisha continued to relay her disapproval at the entire sordid affair. We drove home in stony silence. Yes, she was holding me responsible for the events of that afternoon.

Somehow, she managed to jut her short little muzzle forward in a pout.

Our next appointment was scheduled in four weeks for another round of shots, but it was only a week later that we were walking through the parking lot again for a meeting with Dr. Beck. As I cradled Keisha in my arms, a large lump was growing on the top of her head. Her ears flopped up and down with each step as we drew nearer to another encounter with the medical community.

Curiosity may have killed the cat, but it just sent my dog to what seemed like endless trips to the vet. What was to be the first of many emergency trips had resulted from an enticing electrical cord dangling from the kitchen counter. As Keisha tugged and pulled at the rubber cord, my iron finally gave way and tumbled over the edge, landing on her head. The crash sent me running from the other room to find Keisha, startled and blinking her eyes at the surprise. Although it seemed like it must have REALLY hurt, she didn't find the need to complain about it. She swiped her paw over her face, smacked her lips and went on to investigate the iron to see where she might chew on it.

Alarmed by the lump growing on her head, I called the vet's office, then grabbed my keys and checkbook. Back to the dreaded metal table, more snarls and protestations. Dr. Beck pronounced her fine and we ended with the ritualistic transfer of funds from my not-fine bank account.

We became regular visitors at Dr. Beck's lair and the monetary investment in my little dog, now a plump six pounds, had churned the ether of my bank account. Keisha's explorations found her nibbling the laundry detergent one evening. Taste-testing something was way more fun, and informative, than just sniffing it, I supposed.

Her stomach had rejected the powdered soap over the expanse of my living room, but while scrubbing the carpet I saw a spot of blood swimming in the mess. This was serious.

My car sped through the now familiar route to the doc's office. *You can't die now*, I thought, *I have too much invested in you.* And for a moment, I realized how I would feel if my new companion were to leave me.

Keisha's digestive tract survived that bout of curiosity but the severity of this event did not quell her search for the next dangerous adventure.

As I continued to transfer funds to Dr. Beck, I sought refuge in the time honored mantra of "ignorance is bliss." Raised by a banker, I had been taught the importance of meticulous bookkeeping, the debits and credits neatly lined up, leading to the all-important "Balance" guiding all budgetary decisions.

Truth be told, the state of my financial affairs had drifted quite far from the orderly, responsible format my father had taught. I became completely averse to logging the entries into my checking ledger. My own banking system had always been a reactionary approach, due to my inability to tailor my desires to my paltry income. But now each time I wrote a check, I winced, said a hasty prayer and slammed the checkbook shut as if to block the risk from my mind. I wore the guilt of this irresponsible behavior like Hester Prynne's "scarlet letter."

I knew that at some point there comes a reckoning, though.

The reckoning arrived at 4:15 the next Tuesday afternoon. My personal line on my office phone lit up with a shrill ring. Hoping it was some exciting invitation from a visiting European prince wanting to be shown the sights of Houston that evening, I quickly grabbed the receiver.

"Lily," my father's voice came through the phone. "Are you having some financial problems?"

No night out with royalty for me tonight.

"Why?" I asked, using my best imitation of nonchalance.

"Well, Herb in Bookkeeping just called me. It seems you had a couple of checks come through that were going to be marked 'Insufficient Funds.' When he saw whose account it was, he called me." My father paused and waited for my response.

My cheeks flushed. I swallowed hard. My father had never needed to spank me as a child nor even raise his voice. Confronting me with my own misdeeds usually resulted in me crumbling into a pile of tears and begging for forgiveness. I felt that really wasn't an option here at my desk so I pinched the bridge of my nose to stop the flow of tears and held my breath. The silence on the phone was more than tense.

I never wanted to ask for help and I had worked three jobs to pay my own way through college. I prided myself on resourcefulness and independence. To be caught in such an act of irresponsibility was mortifying to me.

"Herb was nice enough to pull the checks and wait until I could run downstairs and make a deposit into your account."

My father's statement was a simple description of what had just transpired in a bank building 150 miles away. But I knew that what went unsaid was more complex and shameful. In my father's Book of Life, money management was listed under the heading of Ethics and Morals. Writing hot checks was the equivalent of turning tricks in the red light district. And the fact that I had sinned within the walls of his bank added further disgrace and denigration of my character. I was not sure if the fact I had not WILLFULLY bounced a check would help matters. But I gave it a whirl.

"Oh, my goodness," I stammered. "I've had so many vet bills lately ...." Thinking quickly back through the most likely culprit, "...I think my last deposit must not have hit in time."

I didn't even convince myself.

"Well, I've deposited enough to cover the checks. Are there any MORE coming?" His tone had shifted from condemnation to one of near-simmering anger. He was asking if I had any more venial sins to confess. And frankly I wasn't sure.

"No. That's it."

Add lying to my list of turpitudes.

But at this point I just couldn't come clean on the state of my moral corruption. I just needed to end this call before I completely embarrassed myself in front of my co-workers.

"Good," my father said. The awful disapproval still streamed through the phone, but the tone had shifted east of complete denunciation. "PLEASE let me know if you have any more problems before this happens again."

This was not a tender offer of help. It was a firm warning that he must never again learn of my depravities from Herb in Bookkeeping.

"No problem," I said, through pursed lips. Mercifully, I heard the call disconnect.

I gingerly placed the receiver back in its cradle. My arm felt weak. Elbows on the desk, I laid my forehead in the palm of both hands. I took a breath. I felt sick to my stomach. I had not been willing to face up to my risky behavior, and now I had been caught red-handed by the last person I wanted to disappoint.

And Herb in Bookkeeping.

Chapter 7

"Life itself is a haphazard, untidy, messy affair"
— Dorothy Day

Even though it was technically fall, the air was still warm and humid. I stood at my front step where just weeks ago the faceless, would-be intruder had brought terror into my night. I fumbled in my purse for my keys. I was tired after a long day at work and I had already flipped off my heels before walking up the steps. I couldn't wait to remove the rest of my business costume and relax. The stress from my day had metastasized from my brain into little packets of tension that flowed through my veins, stinging and burning. I couldn't wait to get inside, remove the day from my awareness and feel my insides become smooth again.

It's interesting how entrenched we become in the everyday rituals of our lives so that we're not even aware of the normal rhythms, such as walking through the door, putting the purse down, taking off shoes and finally opening up the kitchen doors, held together by a dog leash, and greeting a frantically happy puppy. We are not aware of the normal dance until it is interrupted.

Standing in my stocking feet, I pushed open the front door and found, to my surprise, a little black dog standing on the other side, tail wagging furiously, ears wiggling and tongue sliding out the side of her face. A huge smile spread from ear to wiggling ear.

"Hi!" she beamed.

My heart sank.

Meeting Keisha at the door was an abrupt halt to the normal evening rhythm. There she was, face ablaze with happiness, tail wagging furiously and tufts of something brown and fuzzy scattered through her black fur.

As I stepped over the threshold, my heart sank deeper at another discovery. The wretched brown shag carpet that ran from baseboard to baseboard was now in a pile in the center of the room. The origin of the brown fuzzies scattered through Keisha's fur was now identified—padding that had lain hidden beneath the carpet for at least twenty years. Huge pieces of it had been shredded by the little pup standing in front of me and I could see she had tossed it into the air like confetti. What an after-noon she had. Her tail swished with the pride of her accomplishments—her escape, her ability to pull seven feet of broadloom from its tack strip and then shred and toss the carpet fairy-dust that now covered much of the floor.

It was Mardi Gras in my living room.

I dropped the shoes I had been holding and heard them thump on the wooden sub-floor. At that she leaped toward my shoes, snatched one into her mouth and jumped into the pile of carpet in the center of the room. Tossing my shoe into the air like a circus juggler, she then turned her attention back to the carpet padding. Her game of shred-the-carpet resumed.

Tired and overwhelmed by this scene that greeted the end of a long work day, I slumped into a chair and thought seriously about crying. Those little grains of stress that had been flowing through my veins now made their way to my eyes in the form of stinging tears.

Just weeks before, I had come home to find that Keisha—frustrated with being left alone—had soothed her frayed nerves by chewing on the kitchen cabinets. The aspiring termite discovered the joys of sprawling on the smooth linoleum and putting all her energies into gnawing, from the bottom corners, the old wooden cabinets that were the walls of her daytime prison. Having administered the requisite scolding and dropping what I thought was a smorgasbord of chew toys onto the floor before leaving for work, I hoped (and prayed) that this new pastime would not continue.

The reprimands and the chew-options had done nothing to stop her preferred method of whiling away the hours. The frayed and jagged-edged cabinets were now decidedly shorter than before. As the rising tide of destruction grew, my security deposit was slowly but surely ticking away and it was only time until the pots and pans would be exposed.

How could something so cute and fuzzy be so destructive? I didn't have the money to install new cabinet doors, nor install new carpeting. My bank account was already bleeding and on life support.

My eyes clouded over with hot tears and I welcomed the relief that followed a good cry.

Sensing the shift of emotions coming from my chair, Keisha stopped the carpet demolition with an abrupt bark and jumped up into my lap and began to cover my face in kisses. Just a few days ago she had not been able to jump onto the furniture and now her growing limbs had allowed her to effortlessly sail onto my lap. Her steady growth was making it harder and harder to contain Houdini.

Her determined kisses and happiness at being with me in the chair deflated my mounting sense of overwhelm and despair. The good cry was going to have to wait. I couldn't stop the smile that now seemed to grow on its own across my face. The messy kisses continued and soon I was laughing and hugging her sturdy little body. Keisha had accomplished what very few had ever been able to do: stop the downward spiral of a bad mood in its tracks.

The gloom and overwhelm passed and I hoisted myself from the chair so I could begin the task of cleaning up the mayhem strewn across the room. The carpet was stretched back toward the walls and attached back to the tack strip. My floor now had some interesting potholes where the padding had been removed and shredded. But the day of reckoning with my landlord would come when I moved out.

The list of devastation was growing daily and I wondered if anyone had ever served prison time for excessive damage to a rental.

Chapter 8

"Oh the places you'll go."
— Dr. Seuss

Always searching for new and entertaining things to do with our little ones, Anna and I decided to take a Saturday afternoon and introduce Keisha and Chandon to the ocean. So after a leisurely brunch one Saturday morning, we packed everything we thought we'd need for a great afternoon: food, towels, books, magazines, chairs, sunscreen and a big umbrella—all the necessities to experience the great outdoors. After skillfully filling the trunk with our loot, we loaded *the kids* into the backseat, tucked the leashes into the glovebox and headed down the interstate to Galveston, fifty miles south.

I loved everything about the beach and I couldn't wait to introduce these two to the joys of sand and surf. This would be their first experience of the ocean and all its beauty. The late fall day was proving to be warm. The backseat contingency napped the last half of the drive and slowly awoke once the car pulled onto the soft sand of the beach. Long past the vacation season, the beach was nearly empty, and we cautiously pulled the car to a spot about twenty-five yards from the water line.

The tangy smell of salt filled the car and the sound of the crashing waves heralded our entrance into another world, far away from life in the city. As I looked up through the open sun roof, I could see sea gulls surfing the wind currents and trailing our car, hoping for food. The warmth of the sun felt soft and welcoming on my face. It was going to be a relaxing afternoon. What fun our dogs were going to have!

We piled out of the car and began the laborious task of setting up our camp for the day. Keisha, always lacking any sort of modulation, flew out of the back seat, landed for a very brief moment on the ground and proceeded to do some sort of dance (more like a seizure) of joy as the sights and sounds of the sea surrounded her. I was concerned that she was going to injure herself with the flips and twirls across the sand, but her joy was so comical I couldn't help but laugh.

As Anna and I began to unload things from the back of the car, Keisha continued her spasms and acrobatics in the sand. We soon noticed, though, the rather large furry head of Chandon still in the backseat, sitting completely still and staring ahead.

Anna walked around to the open door and directed, "Come on, Chandon. Come on, boy."

Stony silence met the invitation. No movement from the car.

"Look at Keisha ... look at what fun she's having!" Anna continued, pointing to the chaos now happening beside our car. Spews of sand erupted from wherever the twirling ball of black fuzz traveled. Small chirps of pleasure could be heard from the sandstorm.

I was pretty sure that sighting Keisha's spastic fit was really not the best enticement for the staid Chandon.

His somber face stared resolutely ahead, as if ignoring his surroundings might make them disappear. It seemed clear now that the smell of the salt, the sounds of the waves and the tornado of sand spinning around Keisha's paws had removed any doubt for Chandon that a beach outing was not for him.

If Chandon had been a human, likely he would have lived in a palatial estate in the English countryside. The lord of the manor would spend his time perusing the books in his library, clad in a silk smoking jacket and sipping a Dubonnet on the rocks. Chandon was drawn to the subtle, more sophisticated pleasures of life and his muscular, stocky build belied his delicate nature.

Keisha interrupted her violent celebration for a brief second to see what her friend was up to. Tail wagging furiously, tongue lolling out the side of her mouth, her eyes peered up through the window and sparkled with a clear invitation to her friend to join the fun. Again, it was met with stony silence as Chandon sat Sphinx-like in his bucket seat.

Never one to let someone damper her fun, Keisha left Chandon to his dark cloud and resumed her I'm-at-the-beach dance while Anna and I turned our attention to the problem at hand.

"Maybe this wasn't such a good idea," I said, now beginning to realize this may not be the carefree day we had anticipated.

"He just needs to get out of the car and see where we are, that's all," the ever-optimistic Anna reasoned.

But as Anna's enthusiasm increased, so did Chandon's resolve. We both crawled into the back seat, petted and coaxed. We pulled some of the snacks from our coolers and enticed. Never one for petty tricks or blackmail, Chandon became more repulsed by the entire affair. The English gent braced his jowls and resolved to ride this fiasco out in the comfort of his auto. Physical force was now our only option.

Anna and I clipped on his leash, mustered all of our physical strength and through sheer, jaw-clenching determination pulled the beast from the car.

The car rocked back and forth several times until the final heave-ho and all three of us finally tumbled from the backseat, hitting the sand with a thump. Despite his size, Chandon's agility and gracefulness allowed him to right himself with amazing speed, freeing him from the clutches of two crazed women.

Almost as soon as his paws hit the ground, they practically retracted into his legs at the feel of the gritty, wet sand. His jaw clenched and his eyes squinted unhappily as he stood against the wind that was kicking up stinging particles of sand. The humidity in the air was laden with salt spray, lending a sticky feeling to the wind. His ears twitched as the waves crashed noisily against the beach. This massive canine, whose strength could mortally wound a foe with ease and whose lineage included the revered Chinese temple guards, was frozen in fright against the assault on his delicate senses.

We both stared at Chandon's rigid body, unsure as to what would happen next. While all the drama played out at the car, Keisha's dance of joy had continued, unnoticed. It now moved around the side of the car and took aim at the statue-like Chandon. She sailed through the air, briefly pushing off his left hip with her back paws, and flipping backwards to land beside him.

"Come on, my friend", she seemed to say through the radiant smile that flashed across her face. "The beach is SUCH a great place!" She began to jump up and lick his rigid muzzle, her whiffles and peeps clearly audible over the wind and crashing waves.

This further assault on Chandon made him stiffen even more. He bent his back legs in an effort to sit and solidify his stand but then immediately straightened, realizing it would only increase the surface area in contact with the gritty sand. Keisha's elation was in direct contrast to the misery now being experienced by the love of her life. And she seemed oblivious to his predicament.

"Maybe if we get him in the water, he'll be okay," Anna said, unconvincingly.

Lacking any sort of confidence in this approach, I thought we had nothing to lose. Leaving Anna to handle her pained companion, I called my little whirling dervish to follow me to the water. Eager to explore this great new environment, she sprinted past me and hit the wet part of the sand. Delighted in this new sensation, she set to digging frantically and buried her body in the cool earth. Rolling several times, she hopped back onto her four little legs, sand caked in layers of her thick fur. Snorts and sneezes cleared her nose of the wet sand and she dove in again. The delights of wet sand had stopped our progress to the water in its tracks.

Progress was not being made back at the car either. I could see both parties now firmly entrenched.

I looked out to the sea as the tide began to march closer to me. The waves churned the water and made it dark and cloudy with sand and seaweed. As Keisha gleefully continued her antics in the sand, I began to be concerned about her unbridled joy in the water. Her exuberance might prove dangerous in the fast moving surf.

I scooped up the vibrating ball of fur and looked back at Anna and Chandon, still anchored in their stalemate. None of this was turning out to be the idyllic outing at the beach, so I headed back to the car.

Twenty minutes later we were traveling down the freeway and heading home. The dogs had resumed their respective spots in the back. Anna and I talked most of the way, watching as the sun set, and the dogs remained eerily quiet.

But our conversation soon halted as something was amiss in the backseat. It took a moment for us to realize Chandon was frantically pushing himself up against the back of Anna's seat, in an attempt to squeeze through to the car door. He was desperately trying to escape!

Puzzled and concerned, my eyes swept the back seat to see what was going on and it took a moment to discern the unusual image I now could see (and the cause for Chandon's desperate flight). Backlit by the lights of the cars behind us was the outline of Keisha, poised atop a speaker on the back shelf of the rear window with her back hunched over her rear paws. She was depositing a pile of poop.

Chandon's hygienic sensibilities had been pushed beyond their already short tether. As the poop continued its descent upon the shelf, Chandon's panic increased and he began clawing at the window. Anna, seeing the drama in the rear view mirror, let out a scream and pulled the car to the shoulder immediately. The cars flew past at a deafening rate and we simultaneously opened the doors for immediate ejection. Chandon wasted no time. One hundred and twenty pounds of golden fur catapulted from the door and hurdled across the roadside gulley, landing near a grove of trees.

Once out of the car, I realized I needed to go back and retrieve the culprit. The lights of the oncoming traffic were blinding and made it hard to see in the dark interior of the car, but with every flashing blast of light I could see the same outline of the little puppy against the rear window. It was reminiscent of the silhouette of the black cat against the Halloween moon but this was a more sinister activity. She looked stunned by the turn of events and a bit confused as to what had caused the mass exodus.

I scooped her up from the back ledge and pulled her into the night air. The sound and lights from the interstate were disorienting, but she was more concerned about her backseat companion and his frantic escape. Her tiny black eyes scanned the roadside vegetation and soon found Chandon, who had taken up a post as far from the car as he could without retreating into the woods. He turned his back to us, not wanting to acknowledge that he was in any way associated with the disgraceful events in the car. Keisha, now in my arms as I stood beside the freeway, seemed perplexed as to all the commotion and rejection by her friend.

Chandon came by his cleanliness obsessions honestly and Anna, never without a wet-wipe near, had already swooped in as the hazmat crew. She was amazingly good-natured about the assault on her speakers, but then again Anna was one of those blessed souls who found pleasure in the act of cleaning. She was the proverbial yin to my yang, the Felix to my Oscar. My mind became a bit overwhelmed with the now imminent task of removing puppy poop from a car speaker but Anna jumped in with the determination and concentration of an elite member of the Army bomb-disposal unit.

With the backseat now set to order, our next task was to coax the horror-stricken Chandon back into the car. The mission required a leash, the body strength of two women and a trail of evidence in the vegetation of Chandon's nail-clawing protest against our "persuasion" to return to the car.

Keisha rode in my lap for the balance of the trip, contrite and meek. The indignation and anger from the back seat was palpable.

But Keisha the traveler had arrived.

Chapter 9

> *"I was going to buy a book on hair loss, but the pages kept falling out."*
> — Jay London

By mid-November, the warm, humid autumn days had given way to cooler and overcast weather with Thanksgiving and the holidays just around the corner. Life had become calmer as we settled into our routine. Mornings included Keisha's standing guard at the shower curtain, playing hide-and-seek with my makeup bag (she hid, I yelled and cursed while seeking) and trekking downstairs for her morning bathroom ritual. Evenings included the joyful reunion after work, our evening meal, a nightly walk around the neighborhood, oftentimes with Chandon and Anna, and finally us both tucking into my bed with her rubber pork chop.

Keisha's round, plump body stretched into that of a gangly teenager. Her legs became longer and thinner, her fur became less fuzzy. Her snoot extended in an aristocratic sort of way, her ears longer and less furry, but still flipped forward at the tips.

As the trees outside my windows began to drop their leaves, a similar event seemed to be taking place with Keisha. Her short, fuzzy fur was giving way to longer, finer fur that accentuated her slimmer body. Brushing her fur every evening, I began to notice chunks of it coming out in the brush. Soon small bald patches began to appear and I began to become alarmed.

Over the next few days, the bald patches increased and, though she had plenty of energy, she had the looks of a sickly waif. We headed down the now familiar and well-traveled path to Dr. Beck's and exchanged more hard-earned money for a formal diagnosis: puppy mange. The word conjured images of mongrels scavenging back alleys and living from trashcan to trashcan. But this was my sweet, spoiled and otherwise very healthy baby.

Armed with an ointment and reassurances from the doctor that the scourge would heal, we headed home and a new, terrifying realization took hold of me. The doctor had explained the hair loss was due to a small mite that lived in the environment, the environment that I shared with my now best friend. As I steered the car home, I pictured Keisha snoozing alongside me, mites chomping away at her skin, mere inches from my own scalp. And my own hair.

The relationship with my hair was a long and complicated one. A vivid trauma at the age of six involving a pixie-cut that convinced my mother brought out some hidden beauty, left with me a pathological attachment to my hair and a conviction that it should never be cut above my shoulders. Many forays into trying out new styles and cuts had only ended badly for me, the hairdresser and anyone else that dared suggest that the cut or style looked good. My identity was now deeply invested in having long hair. And in the past year I had let it grow to new lengths; the ends now touched my waistline.

I had also just plunked $100 on my credit card for highlights. I had a lot invested in my hair, both literally and figuratively.

As Keisha slept off the travails of the appointment in the seat next to me, images of my own bald spots, long clumps of hair falling to the floor, and total devastation of my mane all flashed through my mind. By the time we pulled into our parking space, I was almost hyperventilating and had reached the conclusion that this chapter could only end with shaving my head for a final clearing of the destructive mites and needing to relocate to another city until I could re-grow my hair. That would probably take twelve to fifteen months.

Mange. It might have well as been the Black Plague for all the devastation I now was convinced loomed on the horizon.

We plodded upstairs and I collapsed on the couch. Keisha trotted to the water bowl and noisily slurped away, seemingly unconcerned with the catastrophic news we had been dealt. Despite the assurances of the vet, I was sure that I would be forced to confront my unreasonable attachment to my hair. A frantic call to the vet's office and the doctor's explanation that I was indeed safe from bald patches and wispy twigs of hair did little to assuage my anxiety.

My mangy mutt jumped onto the couch and burrowed into my side, emitting a contented sigh. I reflexively reached out and stroked the now sparse, rough fur, imagining the tiny savages living on her skin who were probably taking up residence on my own at this very moment. Perhaps she could convalesce at a safe distance from me.

Oh, I knew it was too good to be true. We were having such fun and I felt like those frozen parts of my heart were beginning to thaw the tiniest little bit. I reached over and buried my face in her belly, despite knowing that tiny vermin had taken residence beneath the surface.

Why did love always come with such risk?

During the next few weeks, we plowed through the medicated baths and the ointment applications that promised to restore her fur and good looks. Thanksgiving had come and gone, my first official holiday where I was not able to be home with my parents. I had to be at work early on the Friday after Thanksgiving and travel was not possible. Some of my extended family gathered at a vacation home a couple of hours outside of Houston and I was invited to join them for the day. Unsure if Keisha was even invited, I knew that it was best not to show up with a diseased-looking dog amidst a food-oriented holiday.

I tearfully left Keisha as I did any other work day, feeling bereft as I drove east along the highway. The beautiful fall colors failed to bring me the joy they normally did, my thoughts (and heart) focused on the lonely little dog spending her first Thanksgiving alone in my kitchen.

The following weekend, Keisha and I tucked into a quiet Saturday evening in our newly Christmas-festooned apartment. Finances being in a dismal state, I had jumped at the opportunity to visit a co-worker's home miles from the urban sprawl and choose, pioneer-style, my first solo Christmas tree from the brush surrounding her home. We chopped the tree down, secured it to the roof of my car and I dragged the spindly plant up the stairs to my waiting dog. Keisha watched as I, with much effort, put the shrub in the stand and placed it ceremoniously in front of the living room window. Store-bought decorations were out of the question, as rent and food were the priority. My mom had donated some lights and I had strung popcorn and ornaments I had cut from paper along the uneven, sparse branches. Keisha and I sat on the floor looking up at our Charlie Brown Christmas tree. I thought, for a moment, that we must have looked comical. Keisha's growth spurt and the slow-healing fur condition had left her looking frail and awkward and our rag-tag Christmas tree, sitting atop the carpet that was secretly missing its foam underpadding, crafted quite a Dickensian holiday scene.

But I felt an unfamiliar wave of happiness at this tender moment. As we sat in the glow of the colored lights, I felt we had survived the last few months of house-training, various health crises and a steady stream of destruction, landing safely in my favorite time of year. I leaned over and petted Keisha's back with a long stroke and kissed her forehead. My heart felt full.

At that moment, the phone rang.

Chapter 10

"Fear is the memory of pain. Addiction is the memory of pleasure. Freedom is beyond both."
— Unknown

Perhaps I shouldn't have picked up the receiver. Perhaps it would have been better to never know the call had made it to my phone. But I answered.

The voice on the other end startled me. And was oh, so familiar.

"Hey, you," *he* said. "What are you doing?" The deep voice on the other end rang in my ear, a voice that had been part of my life for seven years. I thought I had righted myself after so many months of living my new life in Houston. I began to feel myself tip.

"Hi!" I said, stunned. "Not doing much."

The Christmas tree, the lights, the snuggly dog all receded from my awareness. I found myself in quicksand.

"I'm here for the weekend. Staying at the Westin. You wanna meet me for a drink?"

Still caught off guard, I paused, waiting to orient myself to the fact that *he* was on the other end of the phone. And that *he* was literally down the street. And *he* was asking me to come to him.

We met while I was a freshman in college and he had just started his career. That summer we began casually dating but quickly moved deeper into one another's lives in subtle ways, eventually becoming part of the fabric of each other's existence and those of our families. He had felt more like family to me than some with whom I shared DNA. We had toyed with the idea of stepping into "Marriage and Mortgage", as he called it, on more than a few occasions. But as he stepped forward, I stepped back. When I was ready to step forward then his feet moved in the opposite direction. Our dance of back and forth had been long and exhausting.

Looking back, I understood that he and I were drawn together for many reasons. We had totally different backgrounds and upbringings and yet we held vital similarities. Some of those similarities lay under the surface, not seen on the outside, but held deep within so that when they were struck, like a vein of precious metal, it was subtle yet profound. But it was only in retrospect that I could see it. In affairs of the heart, it was the currents that ran beneath the surface that tended to pull me under and threaten my existence.

I felt the current pulling at me again.

"Where are you staying again?" I was trying to bide time till I could get my footing.

"The Westin near the Galleria," he said with ease.

"That's not too far from my apartment," Did he know where I lived? Probably not. He had moved on with ease, I had heard, and probably never looked back. Or so it felt.

"Perfect! Come on over. We can catch up."

After a complete blur of exchange, I hung up the phone and looked at Keisha. She sat expectantly by the tree, waiting for me to come back to her. Her tail wagged, swishing against the carpet. Remorse flooded through my veins, palpable in its heaviness, hot and prickly. Not only had I agreed to drive a few miles to my past, I was leaving my present, a present that had finally emerged from numbing pain to one of simple, furry, Christmas-colored contentment.

Like most addicts, I knew I was slipping backward and it was, most appallingly, a conscious choice. But I still had time to make a U-turn. I looked around the room strewn with chew toys. I saw the door where the faceless intruder had stood, waiting on the other side, several months before. I thought of the fun and laughter that had emerged once Keisha had crossed that threshold. The slow but steady progress that I'd made being pulled by a red leash. I sat frozen. I wanted to cry.

One simple call and I could change the precipitous direction I was heading.

Call and cancel, Lily. Don't go.

If Keisha could talk, would she have said those words? What her eyes were saying was less directive and more inviting—to continue our evening beside one another.

But I pushed the look from my mind and walked to the bedroom to change clothes. I checked my hair and make-up, thinking I wished I looked better. The old, niggling self-doubts were already making their move.

Twenty minutes later I was sitting across from *him*, the noisy bar making conversation difficult. Tears had come as I drove away from my apartment, knowing my little dog was back in her kitchen confinement. I had left the Christmas lights on for her, hoping to continue the festive air for her evening alone. But that image made me all the sadder and the tears became sobs. By the time I arrived at the hotel, I had to reapply my makeup.

And now my eyes, still stinging a bit from the tears, were staring at *his* dark eyes across the table from me. Deeply conflicted, I seemed to stand outside myself, watching. I could see the couple, a rich history situated between one another. And I could see the tiny dog, alone on the linoleum, waiting for her master's return.

I watched his hand curve around the glass dripping with condensation, that dark liquid often between us. It occurred to me that the amber drink in the glass could be just as intoxicating and addicting as the connection that joined us. But alcohol was not my drug of choice.

He was.

I pretended to listen as he spoke about unimportant things but my thoughts ran fast. I hated myself for sitting here, casually sharing a drink with the person who had delivered some serious wounds to my being. I should be home, my new home, nestled on the couch with this wonderful being that entered my life in a time of old pain and new fear. I was a traitor. To myself. To my loyal companion.

And yet the trivial conversation continued despite the glaring undertone that he and I both knew was there. He had always been a master of secrecy regarding his feelings and as usual, I had a hard time discerning where the truth lived. I played my part, as best I could, in the noisy room and we exited the bar close to midnight. Nothing had been said that two people meeting in an elevator wouldn't say to one another on the ride up to their destination. I offered to give him a ride back to his hotel to save him taxi fare. As we got into my car, the unsaid, unnamed, unacknowledged, still-alive connection sat between us and we were silent on the short drive back to the hotel.

I pulled up to the porte cochere of the hotel, warm and lit in the foggy night air. Two bellmen sprang into action and simultaneously opened both our doors. I had planned on dropping him off and was startled when my door swung open, an invitation to exit my seat and enter the hotel.

"Oh," I stammered, being thrown more off kilter than I already was from the evening's turn of events.

"Are you staying the night with us, Madam?" the bellman innocently asked.

I froze.

I slowly turned to face him, still sitting in the passenger seat. He smiled and raised his eyebrows. How many times had I seen that expression?

I pictured my little apartment—Christmas tree and snoozing puppy, all waiting for my return. I breathed in deeply and held my breath.

The addict weighed the options. There was plenty of water in the dog bowl. She had downed a big bowl of kibble for dinner and we had completed our regular nighttime bathroom trip to the front lawn just a couple hours before. If I left now, she'd be happy to see me, but would quickly go back to sleep till morning. The door was securely locked.

Checklist complete, the addict let out her breath and exited the car.

Chapter 11

> *"It is the bungled crime that brings remorse."*
> — P.G. Wodehouse
> Love Among the Chickens

The following week was long and heavy, despite the holiday festivities popping up everywhere. Two steps forward, one step back. But the events of Saturday night felt more like 15 steps back and I was making little headway, it seemed, in gaining lost ground.

Most families harbor secret compartments of resentment and anger for past hurts while many allow them to be flagrantly viewed by anyone willing to look. My new family member, being of a different species, held no such inclination. She easily and naturally looked forward, urging me along with her.

We easily resumed our daily rituals without any notice of the crime that I had brazenly committed. Her love continued to flow, uninhibited, despite my disloyalty, making it all the harder to move forward on my fallen path with any sense of self-respect. Sunday morning had arrived without incident for her and she seemed unfazed by the events.

My transgression had been doubly egregious. I had broken a covenant to myself and at the same time had, in my view, broken some implicit covenant with a being that had poured pure love in my direction.

Addiction is a nasty business.

We continued on with life. Nothing outwardly changed. The phone was quiet, mercifully, as I now could not trust myself to answer it unarmed.

Our evening walks, most often with the sturdy Chandon and lively Anna in tow, now included a show of Christmas lights decorating the lawns. The extra cheer of the holiday did not seem to influence her in any real way as she found walks to be joy-filled excursions on their own merit—no garlands needed. While Chandon maintained a steady but powerful surge forward, Keisha's approach was a panoply of bursts, halts, sniffs, lunges, barks and dives behind my feet should any odd movement off the sidewalk seem menacing.

We wound our way through the residential section of my neighborhood each night and journeyed the final stretch home through the business section, passing store windows decorated with combinations of red and green, silver and gold, blue and white. We ended up each evening at the apartment, the four of us collapsing at the foot of my awkward-looking tree. It felt warm and safe, our little family evenings together. The exercise, the lights, the colors and the camaraderie all seemed to help lift the heavy part of me that remained from that fateful Saturday.

The four of us journeyed together to Austin for the actual holiday, which was quiet and restful. The drive had been uneventful despite Chandon's concern. Anna dropped us off at my parent's house just as Christmas Eve entered its celebratory stretch. My mom and dad began to look forward to seeing Keisha and provided quite a spread of gifts under the tree for such a small creature. Christmas Eve continued to feel magical to me despite my age and as Keisha and I crawled into my childhood bed, I held her close and listened intently for any sign of Santa on the roof. Chew toys, balls, treats and a new collar all arrived from Santa the next day and the holiday wound down with intervals of food, naps and football. We returned to our little apartment (seriously altered now from the mayhem of puppy teeth, claws and pee) and resumed our normal schedule as we moved into the New Year.

The New Year held little of the promise that I used to so enjoy with the turning of each calendar page. The crispness of the cold air, the inviting blank pages of the new calendar and the anticipation of new adventures seemed to be overshadowed by gray, wet skies and a general discomfort in my body. I walked each weekday morning from the parking garage, across the walkway suspended above the busy city street and up the elevator 49 stories above the earth to my little cubicle. I began to dread each step that took me closer to what seemed a confinement of sorts. The grayness permeated the building and the chill did little to warm my mood.

When my boss, who inhabited one of the coveted corner offices with floor to ceiling windows, left for a lunch appointment, I would often sneak into his office and stand in front of the window, looking out over the busy downtown. The view was dense, compact and had a sense of disorder despite the grid pattern of the streets. My eyes lifted past the traffic and skyscrapers and looked toward the horizon.

That side of the building faced south but the horizon offered no view of the Gulf of Mexico, which I knew was only about 50 miles from where my feet were planted. I stood atop a building in the middle of downtown Houston, but I longed for the expansiveness of the ocean, the softness of the sand and the feel of the ocean air. Keisha knew the joys of that place, too.

While I felt imprisoned in the four walls of my office Keisha, too, was contained in the four walls of our kitchen. Each day Keisha settled into her kitchen-home with her towel and toys—her nine to five job.

Her real assignment, though, began with my arrival home. A robust reunion of joyous eeps and peeps, a hearty meal and brisk walk followed each evening. We nestled into the bed each night and I often thought about that night, mere months before, where I had awakened to the sound of the would-be intruder.

Despite the now familiar connection with Keisha, along with the comforting rituals we had forged, I couldn't shake the heaviness and dissatisfaction that had seemed to take hold during the holidays. I couldn't seem to see my future with any clarity while my 'present' felt in some way unsettled and lacking color, as if a dark veil hung over my world. At the very least, I was living in a black-and-white movie.

The winter months marched on with more rain and cold and despite the dismal atmosphere, Keisha's body thrived and her fur now shone with a thick, black luster. She was approaching twenty-five pounds, which was quite an improvement from the spindly figure of the past fall, but she didn't appear to be moving towards the heavy, solid size of Chandon. My home security system appeared to be a petite model.

But her eyes sparkled, her deep-pink tongue often hung lop-sided from her snoot as her lips stretched across her teeth in what appeared to be an ear-to-ear grin. Her tipped ears often sprang to life when her focus shifted to something that intrigued her. Her vibrancy was contagious.

As the winter months hovered over Houston and the rain and gray skies permeated the days, my college-roommate and beloved friend Charlotte returned from a six-month trip to Australia. Oh, how I had missed her! We had met during our sophomore year and life, it seemed, had made sure we found one another. In a campus of more than fifty thousand students, she and I shared three classes together that fall semester and we took the cue by reaching across the large auditorium to introduce ourselves. A native New Yorker, she made me laugh with her dry and quick wit. My own sense of humor often felt misunderstood by others in the Lone Star State.

Maybe it was the heat. Or the humidity. Regardless of local climate conditions, our meeting was kismet.

She had lived in the little apartment on Lake Street for many months before I moved to Houston, and I took residence of the space as she left to explore the southern hemisphere. I missed her presence dearly and felt relieved when she returned and resumed her place once again in the funny old apartment with Keisha and me.

Keisha, too, was more than happy to bring in another member of the household. Charlotte and I quickly fell back in step with our morning coffee klatch, binges of Toll House cookies and raucous midnight gab sessions. Keisha joined right in and brought her own contributions to the Girl's Club.

Most weekday mornings we rousted ourselves from sleep in the pre-dawn hours to exercise before work, joining Anna and Chandon at a midway point. Keisha and Chandon trudged silently in the lead as Charlotte, Anna, and I huffed and puffed behind them along the quiet, dark sidewalks of our neighborhood. It was good to be part of a pack. It felt good to belong, to be supported, and to have daily rituals.

Life seemed brighter after the gloominess of the New Year, and the human members of our pack decided to begin a weekly painting class with Charlotte's mother, a local artist. Anna, Charlotte, and I gathered each Wednesday evening in Peggy's studio for a six-week course in abstract art while Keisha was shuttled over to Chandon's apartment where he braced himself for an evening with the besotted teenager.

My previous art instruction had been more traditional, sketching lines to recreate an image that existed in real life. Abstract art was all new to me: blocks of color, swaths of lines that moved across the page without conforming to anything recognizable.

One evening Peggy asked us to section our canvas into six boxes. In each box we were instructed to paint, with only two colors, an emotion. We all stared blankly at the two rows of three boxes. The confusion and resistance was palpable. But we each took a deep breath and dove in. The room was quiet as we pushed the paint across the canvas, letting it glide across the page in whatever direction it chose. Soon the six boxes were filled and we began to look beyond our own to each other's.

"That looks like sadness" I said, pointing to Charlotte's box of dark brown and deep yellows.

"Is that laughter or maybe joy?" Anna asked, looking to my box of purple with specks of red.

It was intriguing to guess the intent behind each other's creations and to engage with whatever message the colors might hold. The final exercise that night was to paint in a similar way but to collaborate with one another.

I grabbed my brush and dipped it into the blue paint. The color traveled across the paper in a bold splat and then became soft and mottled as it moved towards the edge. I grabbed another brush and swept a bright swath of yellow through a section of the blue and allowed the yellow to stand alone on some of the blank sections of the page. Where the two met, a lime green color emerged.

Charlotte, who had been silently watching the process, took her cue and grabbed a bottle of dark blue, almost black, paint and squeezed a flourishing line across the page that looped in the center and then seemed to travel off the page. We both stepped back and looked at the painting. The collaboration had created an interesting and visually pleasing piece. The mixing of the two energies, the combination of the colors had conspired to create something that was just as pleasing as a traditional painting.

Later that night as I settled into bed, I couldn't stop thinking about how blobs of color, irregular lines and basic disorder on the canvas still yielded something delightful, beautiful even. How the collaboration with another artist created a piece that was even more unique, as well.

I loved collaboration. It was exhilarating and joined one another in a meaningful way. I think I loved the connection the most. I missed that feeling of connection and collaboration with *him*. Our relationship was a unique entity of its own, a mingling of two separate beings to form something that had not existed before. But it was gone. It wasn't erased. It just existed in the past.

And we were all in the present.

But I reminded myself that romantic relationships were only one flavor of that distinctive, commingling of energies. Friends, family members, crazy puppies could all feed that need for collaboration. Just as the lessons in abstract art had opened my eyes to a different view of beauty, I had the inkling that love and connection took many shapes and forms and may have been as beautiful as a messy abstract painting.

The spring months had arrived and with it the approach of my twenty-seventh birthday. Birthdays had always held a special place in my heart. My father had cultivated that space by making each birthday a veritable lottery of delights. He often would take the day off from work and remind me that we had the entire day to do whatever I wanted. Such extravagance was solidly in contrast to my family's normally frugal and ascetic approach to life, and it created great anticipation of the event. The heaviness I felt that past two months seemed to lighten its grip as my birthday month made its entry, along with sunshine and a riot of colors in the flower bed beneath Apartment Six.

Just as my world was brightening and the days moved closer to my birthday weekend, the phone rang with *his* familiar voice on the end.

"What plans for your birthday this year?" He knew how important the day was to me.

I hesitated before offering the information.

"I think I'm coming to Austin for the weekend." I could practically hear the information land on the other end.

"How about I make some dinner Saturday night. Reed is coming over and we can eat, watch a movie and have a little reunion."

Reed was a friend of ours and I hadn't seen him in a while. A third-party presence seemed to make the encounter less dangerous.

"That sounds fun. Let me check, though, with Anna and see what she has planned." No need to commit yet, I thought.

The call ended and my mood teetered on the edge between the lightness I had begun to feel and the dark heaviness that had lain across my shoulders all winter. I grabbed the leash, clipped it on the red collar that now extended to its full expansion, and headed out for a nice long stroll in the sunshine. Our walks had become a boon to my soul. As Keisha's limbs grew so did the length of our outings. We traversed neighborhoods, parks, hiking trails and even shopping centers. She had a natural talent for matching her pace with my own and rarely pulled or stopped the forward movement along our path now that she was a bit older. We were most often in perfect step with one another. The fresh air seemed to clear my head and my mood.

Why not, I thought. This could be an opportunity to leave the past. To finally move beyond the pain that had seemed to bubble to the surface after our last encounter at the hotel.

A few phone calls to friends in his circle unearthed vital information that he was seeing someone, although she currently lived out of state. Maybe he was hoping to clear the past, too, so that we could both move fully into the next phase of our lives. This would be a great opportunity to accomplish that goal that had yet to be verbalized by anyone.

I looked down at my non-verbal companion, panting and smiling from the walk, back legs splayed across the kitchen linoleum. As I gazed into the shiny black eyes, I felt a wave of love. Whether she sensed my internal rationalizations or the treacherous path ahead, I couldn't tell. Living in the moment was a dog's forte and nature seemed to be in full bloom here. I took her cue and splayed on the kitchen floor, too. From that vantage point, the future didn't seem to matter right now.

Chapter 12

> *"Who has not sat before his own heart's curtain? It lifts: and the scenery is falling apart."*
> — Rainer Maria Rilke

My birthday always marked the beginning of *my* New Year. And this year I hoped for a dramatic shift in the momentum and direction of my life. The dinner I had agreed to attend that night held high hopes in my mind for a tangible shift in the winds. I passionately wanted to move into a new, happy, exciting phase of my life—my destiny, even. And it felt like unresolved feelings were strapped to my back, to my heart and even to my feet. Keisha and I may have logged countless miles on our walks but I felt like I was going nowhere.

The day had been a picture-perfect spring day—warm and sunlit, with the smell of freshness and growth. Keisha and I stood on the front porch of *his* new condo as the day began to shift to evening. I could feel my heart beat in my chest as I held the leash tightly. It felt good to have my personal protection contingency by my side.

The door opened and *he* greeted me with a casualness that I could not muster. I walked into the space, unfamiliar to me just as his life had become unfamiliar to me. I could smell something wonderful coming from the kitchen. Reed had already arrived and leapt from the couch to give me a bear hug. A welcome reunion and another guard to protect me!

While I felt completely uncomfortable and uneasy in the setting, Keisha trotted around the room inspecting each crevice and corner as if she owned the place. I eyed her movements as the three of us talked and reminisced about our time together. He didn't seem to mind the companion I had brought with me; he let her have the run of the house. Not timid by nature, she explored the first floor while we began dinner and later settled comfortably on the fireplace hearth while we started the movie. All seemed to be going well.

The movie ended, dinner dishes put away, and conversations exhausted, Reed exited the condo with a quick, side-long glance at me. I caught the look but opted not to hold onto it.

It was just the two of us now.

"You don't have to drive home. You can stay here tonight," he said. I thought I caught a glimmer of nervousness in his eyes.

I wondered what his girlfriend would think of that. But she was miles way away, I guess.

"What about Keisha?" I said, throwing out an obstacle to see where it landed. "I'm not sure I'd trust her to roam free in a place she doesn't know."

I eyed the new carpeting and thought of the potential damage.

"I still have a crate from mom's puppy," he offered. "It's in the garage".

Ten minutes later, after a cacophony of crashes and bangs, he emerged from the garage with a dog crate.

One obstacle was gone, but would Keisha serve up another?

No such luck. She pranced into the crate, circled a couple of time, plopped down and ceremoniously tucked her snoot under her tail.

I sighed. My head knew that I should take my exit—birthday celebration complete, now head home. But my heart and some deeper part I could not identify ached to stay. To tuck, snoot to tail, into the comfort of my past. To nuzzle up to something that I missed. My head told me it wasn't there anymore. My heart argued that I could bring it back.

The debate raged as I walked upstairs.

The morning sunlight streamed through the window. I was disoriented at first. My birthday, the dinner, the walk upstairs. And Keisha! I sat bolt upright and raced through the bedroom door. There, at the foot of the stairs, was a scene that caused me to stop dead in my tracks.

The crate sat on the landing, door open and a towel halfway pulled out. Keisha sat Buddha-like, her behind firmly planted on the bottom step, staring up into his face, enraptured. He sat next to her on the same step, elbows on his knees, clad comically in a set of boxer shorts, his uncombed hair sticking up in an array of spikes. They turned towards one another as he carried on some deep conversation with the shiny little black dog that had stolen my now broken heart. And she, in turn, listened intently to the man who had caused it to break.

The scene was intimate and sweet and I felt like a voyeur. I could feel my heart begin to ache—an ache I could not understand, but knew wasn't good. Standing at the top of the stairs, I realized I had placed quite a layer of armor around myself despite crossing the threshold last night and ultimately walking up the stairs. But now that armor seemed to slip away, flimsy as silk. I was dangerously vulnerable and I was in a land that was both familiar and yet entirely foreign.

I could not allow these two to connect.

As Keisha sat next to him, she had brought out the side of him that had captured my heart and held it prisoner all those years. I had worked long and hard to escape its grasp.

I backed away from the door. Bumping into the dresser, I noticed a jewelry box sitting in the center. I opened it and saw woman's jewelry laid out in the individual compartments. The earrings and the necklaces were proof of the danger alarm I had felt so piercingly in the doorway.

It was time for Keisha and me to leave.

Even though I wanted to cry, I held in the tears the entire drive home. I crawled into bed and, finally, cried until I fell asleep. I awoke from my fitful sleep and the tears resumed with a vengeance. My birthday, my favorite day of the year, had become dark and heavy. My bones felt tired. I felt disoriented and completely, numbingly unhappy.

My twenty-seventh birthday found me questioning how I could feel so much discomfort, so much dissatisfaction, so much confusion. I had always been strong and plowed through life with a sense of purpose and optimism. My path had always seemed clear. And yet here I was on the twenty-seventh anniversary of my entry into the world, standing in a place I did not necessarily want, in a funny old apartment, in a job where I felt trapped, with a constant flow of money problems and a heart that longed for a connection that promised more pain than pleasure. I had no clear goals. No clear desires.

I was searching for my place in the world.

Who was I and where did I belong?

I thought about my desk at work, waiting for tomorrow so I could step into the confines of my cubicle. I spent eight or nine hours a day analyzing *Return-on-Investment* spreadsheets that determined whether something was a good investment or not.

I thought of my friends, my same age, who were already building a kind of equity in their life—a job they valued, a romantic relationship that was supportive and nurtured them, marriage, children, or even just a continuation of their studies to broaden their work. They were all forging a path, it seemed to me, that had substance, value. They were investing in their future, their lives. But I felt none of my investments so far had panned out well. My diploma hung on the wall, a testament to hard work and achievement, but had done little to garner any sort of real career. My seven-year relationship, where I put the majority of my energy and focus, was gone with very little to show for it other than a bruised heart that was on lock-down. I didn't even have divorce papers to give any legality to my loss.

My initial investment of $75 for Keisha had morphed into a continual expenditure of cash, almost daily requirements of more capital. Yet I suspected, even in my dismal mood now, it may turn out to be my best investment so far. Some investments are slow-growth and high yield.

But how did I end up here? I looked back along the path. It was a series of decisions, most definitely. But were those decisions made by me? By someone else? And if I made them, what were they based on? My beliefs or someone else's? Did I make them out of fear? Out of convenience?

The questions swirled in my head and made the disorientation worse. I could hear Keisha's whiffles as she slept beside me. I buried my face in the fur of her belly and my tears soaked her soft, black coat.

There was something pure and settling about the feel of her warm belly. I breathed in and my breath stuttered. It woke her and she moved her head, so that her tongue could lick my face. She tenderly lapped at my salty cheeks, her tongue rough and warm. I welcomed the consolation that she lovingly offered.

I had reached some sort of turning point, here in the dark, in the bed where I had awakened months before, to the sound of the would-be intruder. The stranger never entered the apartment, but my unhappiness now filled the space. I closed my eyes, holding onto Keisha, unsure as to what my next step would be.

Where is all this taking me? Where is *my* place in the world?

The only thing I knew for sure: there was a sweet, but irascible little dog beside me. She settled in beside my rib cage and sighed.

We both closed our eyes and drifted off to sleep.

Chapter 13

*"Life is like a dogsled team.
If you ain't the lead dog,
the scenery never changes."*
— Lewis Grizzard

The universe seemed to be eavesdropping that night. It must have heard my cries and understood my longing for something, anything, to change. I was standing at a crossroads and a path was now slightly in sight.

It was ironic that the universe delivered its assistance via Jonathan, or Hamlet as I now secretly thought of him. Only eight months ago he had delivered a dark summation of my future with Keisha—Heartache City. And now he had an offer that was bright, optimistic and intriguing.

The call had come Saturday morning, two weeks after my dismal birthday celebration.

"I'm moving to California this summer, right before I'm scheduled to take the bar, and then I don't start work 'til late September. I've planned a trip around the world before I start work." He paused for dramatic effect. "How would you feel about helping me move? Then you can house-sit for me while I'm gone?"

Law school graduation was near and he had been interviewing with firms for several months. The job market in Texas was still bleak and only a few days before he had accepted a position from a firm in San Diego. His excitement was contagious.

"I know you've wanted to move to California for a while," he said. "Here's your chance!"

I indeed had several job-hunting trips to the West Coast the last couple years that ended in a few job offers, but I had yet to muster the courage to make the move. Now it felt different.

Still taking in his words, I glanced over at Keisha. Her head and front legs were buried under the covers of my unmade bed, and her back paws stretched out in a kind of acrobatic split. I could hear her munching on her plastic pork chop.

"Wow, that's quite a proposition," I said. The words felt like a huge understatement. It took a moment to digest this information.

We talked a bit more of logistics and the next few weeks continued the dialogue. I mulled through the pros and cons, ever the cautious one making lists and running the numbers. I took long walks with Keisha by my side and contemplated what seemed on the surface to be a selfish, impetuous move. I was neither impetuous, nor prone to putting my needs above another, but something was pulling me.

Six weeks after my fateful birthday, I decided I was ready to take the leap.

That leap took me from our little apartment in the dense urban noise of Houston to the open highway of west Texas, headed to San Diego and an unknown future. The road was endless, and the sun baked the landscape as my car headed west. The thermometer on the dashboard read 112 degrees. The noon sun bleached the Arizona desert into a landscape painting of browns and rusts. I had never liked the desert. My soul longed for the ocean and deep blues reflected from the sky. But I was traveling now though the starkness of the terrain to arrive at an uncertain next few months, at the edge of the continent.

The decision to head west had turned out to be a relatively easy one given the current discomfort of my life. I was not really tied to anything. I had proceeded conservatively as I had always done and taken a leave of absence from my job. I had put my belongings in storage, and had worked a second job to have a cushion in my bank account. A garage sale added more funds to my safety net. No stone had been left unturned.

I was to live in Jonathan's apartment, rent-free, for the next two months while he traveled around the globe—a law school graduation gift.

It had all fallen into place fairly easily except for one thing: Keisha.

Jonathan's apartment, my free living space, did not allow pets. Rents in southern California were significantly higher than Texas; I felt I couldn't pass up the chance to plant stakes in my new city rent-free. So I had decided that Keisha would stay behind while I ventured out. I had no plan other than I would see what presented itself. I didn't know if I would stay beyond the two months or continue indefinitely. This strategy was completely new for me. For the first time in my life I was really stepping out into the unknown.

Many of my friends and colleagues shared my excitement while others raised a cautious brow. I was sensitive to both and the battle between the two was strong within me as well. My new best friend, my roommate, walking partner and soulmate gave me no indication of how she viewed the latest development. I experienced great sadness when I thought of leaving her. We were just getting started, after all. But life had presented an opportunity I could not pass up and at a time that I shuddered to think would go on without a change.

I hugged her close and whispered in her ear about my plans. Her eyes watched my lips move and she gave me a quick couple of licks on my face. They say dogs live in the moment and from what I had seen this appeared to be true. No calendars to look forward at future dates. No photo albums or journal to document the past. Just this moment.

I scratched her ears and kissed her forehead. I would only leave her for a short while and like an immigrant booking passage to a new country, I would send for my family member to follow later.

As predicted, my mother fiercely stated that she would not watch Keisha for me in my absence. Although my parents had grown to enjoy Keisha, my mother saw the need for much tending to the still young and often mischievous pup. Finally, I arranged for Keisha to stay with my friend Ali, who lived in Austin and was the proud owner of a young Lab named Molly. Ali was far less structured than I and tended to roll with the punches, so I felt they would be a good match for Keisha's temporary housing.

The departure day arrived and I was queasy with a mix of excitement and dread. The final step before pointing my car west would be to drop Keisha off at Ali's (and an eager playmate, Molly). I had packed all her belongings, food and water bowls, blanket, rubber pork chop and chew bone. They were tucked into a paper bag along with her leash and a check to cover food for a couple of months. Keisha trotted into Ali's house with her standard clip and eagerly joined Molly on Ali's new couch. The scene brought me comfort against the wave of sadness and abandonment I projected onto her.

I left Ali's house with a lump in my throat after hugging my little girl and planting a long intense kiss on her forehead. Quiet tears fell all the way back to my parents' home, where I would wait for Jonathan to swing by and form our caravan westward.

The tears flowed again as I waved to my parents standing in the driveway. They both struggled with watching their only child move 1,500 miles away and knowing that I was stepping into a powerful moment in my life. I cried along the first thirty miles of our journey, thinking of Keisha, my companion, now relocated to a home she didn't know and of my parents, hoping this would be a short adventure.

Once the tears had given way, I settled into the journey. Highway 71, connecting Austin with Interstate 10, was winding and hilly, filled with farms, ranches and quaint little towns. It was the Texas that I knew, the landscape of my childhood.

Once we turned onto I-10 the passing scenery took on a different flavor. Whereas the first leg of our journey quietly wound its way, unobtrusively, through the countryside, I-10 plowed through the land with a loud presence. The road advanced into the Texas desert, refusing to yield to the natural landscape. It sliced through the hills, creating rocky cliffs on either side. The energy of the road grabbed me and took me quickly on my journey west.

It didn't occur to me until later that night, unable to sleep due to the whistling of the old motel air conditioner, that the journey so far was symbolic of this bold decision. I needed at this point in my life some space, to shake off the past a bit, right myself and figure out a plan. I needed clear eyes, not ones clouded by tears, regrets or self-doubt. I just needed breathing-room and a moment to center and ground myself.

For the next 16 hours, my eyes scanned the expanse of the deserts of Texas, New Mexico and Arizona, never-ending miles of sand and rock. The mesas resembled slumbering, ancient giants on the horizon and offered a hint of the elevation that soon came into view. As the road climbed steeply up the mountains outside of San Diego, the temperature dropped dramatically, the desert shifted to rocky elevations and finally descended to the edge of the farthest point west you can go and still stay dry.

What and who might be waiting for me on this adventure?

The July day was sunny and cool by Texas standards and I was in awe of the crispness to the air, informed by winds traveling across the vast Pacific Ocean. To my amazement the apartment that Jonathan had rented did not have air-conditioning (a must in Texas), but I soon learned that we didn't need it. Things *did* feel different here!

The long journey had been an opportunity to cast aside, mile by mile, the life I was leaving and to step into whatever was to play out. And yet a tiny part of me stayed dialed in to the space where my little black dog was hanging out. I called Ali as soon as we arrived. There was no answer and I left a message with my new number. I felt a pang in my heart when I thought of her and how I missed her.

I hoped she did not feel similar discomfort.

Jonathan and I set about getting things sorted and unpacked. The only items I had brought with me were my clothes, an embarrassing number of shoes, and my coffee maker: the essentials for any new adventure. The movers, carrying Jonathan's belongings, had arrived within hours of our own arrival, and we began the job of sifting and sorting through my friend's boxes. The plan was to get the apartment settled, then help Jonathan study for the bar exam scheduled the next week. The following day he would leave on his month-long trip, and I would be left alone in my new city to forge who-knew-what adventure.

Ali called with updates that Keisha and Molly were doing well. I missed our daily walks with her tremendously and I continued them in her absence. But I began to delight in exploring my new city. I felt lighthearted and invigorated by searching out those new staples of life—the supermarket, the closest gas station, restaurants, cleaners, a great coffee house. They would eventually become mundane, but now it was all new.

The nester in me was now fully engaged.

On the third day in San Diego, I stepped into the apartment after my walk on the beach, still feeling the effects of the calming blue water. Jonathan sat at the table amidst stacks of books and notes for his exam, looked up and said, "Ali called. You need to call her back as soon as possible."

My heart sank. Something was wrong! I quickly grabbed the phone and dialed the number. My imagination ran wildly to an array of dire circumstances as Ali picked up the receiver.

"Lily, I'm afraid to tell you," my pounding heart began to hurt. "...things are not going so well here."

Oh God.

I was being punished for being selfish and doing something as reckless and careless as this. My irresponsibility had caused something to happen to Keisha.

"Keisha is completely out of control. She has taught Molly how to escape through the back fence and I've had to round them up several times. She has gotten into the garbage three times now and strewn it everywhere." She took a breath and my heart began to calm just the tiniest bit.

"Then this afternoon," she said, her voice became a bit breathy, "she and Molly escaped to some mud puddle and came back in and landed straight on my new couch."

I could picture the crisp white linen couch and how it must currently look. I could hear it in Ali's voice. My normally unflappable friend had been dealt circumstances where she needed to draw the line.

I continued to listen.

"I think," she said, hesitating before continuing. "This is not working out." She stopped and I could feel her empathy for the situation even while the muddy paw prints were still drying on the white linen.

"She is so full of spunk and mischief." She went on, trying to explain the decision and to soften the news. "She's teaching Molly all sorts of bad habits."

I knew the next line.

"I think you need to come and get her."

I let out a sigh. She was alive. The wave of relief was swiftly followed by the next level of drama. I was 1,500 miles away. I knew something had to be done quickly before more destruction took place and Molly had completely converted to a juvenile delinquent.

"Let me see who I can arrange to come get her," I said, trying to think out loud.

"Okay," she replied.

I could hear the concern for me in her voice along with a couple of yips and barks that could only belong to my girl. I sighed and looked down at the sand that still clung to my bare feet. The peace I felt beside the ocean only an hour ago was gone. I picked up the phone and a few calls later, I was forced to plead and essentially beg my dad to drive over and get my errant dog. My dad had always been an understanding and generous father and he took pity on my plight. My mother, on the other hand, was often firm in her stands and I knew that a destructive puppy was something my mother would not tolerate. But I had no other option. I reluctantly put my dad in the position of breaking the news to my mother. I relayed Ali's directive that he could pick Keisha up within the hour. I would never know exactly how the news was presented to my mom, but I knew the bullet my dad had taken for me.

He was indeed on Ali's doorstep within the hour, collecting Keisha's things and placing her in the passenger seat of his truck. I had stepped out for dinner and missed his call. The message was short and crisp. Keisha was safely at their house and seemed fine. The brevity of the message indicated that Keisha was happy.

My mother, however, was not.

Chapter 14

"The mind that perceives limitation is the limitation."
— Buddha

The adventure started with a rough beginning, but as Keisha settled into my childhood home, I began navigating my new city. It felt like Christmas each day, having access to the ocean, and I spent much time sitting in front of the expanse of blue. It sparkled and moved in hypnotic waves. The Pacific Ocean had a completely different feel from the Gulf Coast where I spent time as a child—the deep blue color, the cool, crisp air and the golden sunlight. It felt magical to me, almost as if Walt Disney had instructed his artists to create it.

I missed my daily routines with Keisha and I desperately missed her presence. I missed her snuggling in the crook of my legs at night. I missed her tail wagging furiously with glee as I poured the kibble. I missed the softness of her fur. So many tangible things I missed about the now thirty-pound dog. But what I missed most was intangible. I missed her essence.

It was light and playful. It sparkled in a way similar to the beautiful ocean I visited every day now. I wanted to share my new adventure with this furry being that had become part of me. Moving to an area where I knew no one offered delicious amounts of quiet time along with the ability to do whatever I wanted whenever I wanted. I had phone calls with my parents and various friends to update them on how things were going but for the most part I found I had few conversations with anyone. In some ways, it felt a bit like a silent retreat.

The absence of conversation seemed to allow me to hear my own inner conversations more fully. It was both revealing and appalling to hear those inner voices. At times they were excited and hopeful; other times they were fearful and negative. The silence and the solitude were soothing but on more than one occasion slipped into loneliness.

When those times hit I often would get in the car, put on my favorite music and head to the beach. I never felt alone when I looked out at the vast expanse of the water. The little village of La Jolla sat due west of Jonathan's apartment and her streets were lined with art galleries, shops and restaurants. La Jolla is Spanish for "The Jewel" and her sparkling coastline lived up to her moniker. I often parked my car and walked along the shoreline or along the streets of La Jolla amidst the tourists and sunburned shoppers. The air was thick with the smell of the seaweed and suntan lotion. It felt like a holiday.

I walked down the bustling street of Girard, and came upon The Cove Theater. Its 1950s exterior harkened back to another time. The marquee letters marched across the front of the building: "When Harry Met Sally." I looked at my watch—10 minutes to the discounted matinee. I stepped inside the cool, dark theater and treated myself to a box of chocolate mints and the story of two people who deal with the question of whether men and women can just be friends. It was sweet and funny, and added to my "vacation" feeling.

For some reason I was drawn to the movie and returned time-and-time again to sit in the old theater and spend two hours with Harry and Sally. Maybe it was Sally's Pollyanna-ish outlook that spoke to the part of me that longed to see the world through such rose-colored glasses. But Harry was unapologetic about his dark side and wore it proudly.

"I have just as much of a dark side as the next person," Sally exclaimed.

"When I buy a new book," Harry countered, "I read the last page first. That way, in case I die before I finish, I know how it ends. That, my friend, is a dark side."

Harry and I were kindred spirits.

No matter how many times I watched the movie I never failed to delight when those two characters ended up together. Maybe it reassured me that one day I might find my other half or that those two aspects of me might join forces and live happily ever after.

With Jonathan off on his travels, I settled into my new surroundings and began to orient myself, still unsure as to what lay ahead. The change in scenery urged me to try new things and I signed up for a painting class downtown by the bay. Peggy's abstract class in Houston had sparked something in me. Each Tuesday we met for three hours as the instructor taught us to use the thick oil paints to create, on our square of white canvas, a replica of whatever was our model or chosen images. One night we chose our subject from a pile of magazine pictures. I leafed through the stack of glossy papers and finally settled on a dark forest scene: a one-lane dirt road curved to the right and disappeared into the inkiness of the trees.

As we stood at our white canvases, our instructor asked us to grab our picture and, before we clipped it to the easel, "turn your picture upside down, please."

Puzzled, we all flipped our magazine page on its head.

"THAT is what you are going to paint. Clip that to your easel and paint EXACTLY what you see."

The confusion of the students filled the studio. She seemed to expect the reaction and continued.

"As an artist, you are going to draw only what you see, not what you think you see. By drawing an upside-down picture, your drawing will be more accurate: your brain will only see lines, shapes and shadows as they relate to one another. It won't see what your rational mind recognizes as a plant, a bridge, a face, an ocean. Placing the picture upside-down gives you the gift of seeing the picture without any context or meaning you impose on it. It will make your job easier as an artist."

There was murmuring amongst us artists. This was new territory.

"Your mind can get in the way of seeing what is really there," she added.

Intrigued, I looked at my upside-down forest and country road. No, I didn't see trees or a road or foliage. My landscape had been replaced by lines that ran vertically across the page. There were various shades of browns and rich greens and blues. A band of gold swerved in the middle of the page and narrowed, until it converged in a point as it approached the darkest area of the vertical lines. I was seeing the scenery from a different vantage point. My mind struggled to make out trees and the road, but it actually felt freeing to see what was there. No meaning. No interpretation. No story.

Being liberated from my struggles with thoughts and pre-conceived notions of my subject, my painting was complete in about twenty minutes. My hand was freed to paint only what my eyes saw, not what I thought was there, not lassoing my rational mind to include all my notions of my subject. Or to try and meet expectations.

I turned my canvas right-side-up and *tada*: the landscape appeared.

That night as I drove home to Jonathan's apartment, I played with this new lens offered by my teacher. I noticed the freeway consisted of lines that ran parallel to one another. The grays became darker as they moved outward. I looked at the hills on either side, not hills but swaths of dark greens interspersed with splotches of browns, even some purples and reds.

It was somewhat disorienting to play this game of *notice what you see, not what you know is there*.

It felt odd to let go of what my logical mind knew was there and see things from the perspective of light, dark, shadows, lines. It felt a bit like I was doing this with life as well. Leaving things that were familiar, and that I probably wasn't seeing clearly anymore, allowed me to see the world around me from a fresh perspective.

I imagined all the landscape between San Diego and Austin—how I might see it from this new perspective. And I wondered how Keisha was doing at the other end of that landscape.

Keisha was settling into her new environment, which had been my home for over 20 years. As an only child, I had no peer that shared space with me—what it was like to live with my parents, Alice and George. Keisha was now stepping into the role I had occupied for years.

My mom had recovered relatively quickly from the responsibility thrust upon her that night. It may have had something to do with Keisha's charms (although that hadn't been enough to keep her residence at Ali's). My mother stood barely over five feet tall, but her presence was commanding. Perhaps this was just what a wild-child dog needed.

As things settled on my end and Jonathan embarked on his own adventure, I was left to address the next piece of my move—finding employment. I detested job hunting. It conjured every self-doubt dormant in my body. Only a few years out of college, I still did not have any breadth of experience that would impress an employer and the economy was not strong. So on my first Sunday morning in San Diego, I woke early, and headed down to the beach with a large cup of coffee and the Sunday classified ads. I found an empty bench in a small grassy area overlooking the rocky shoreline and sat for a moment taking in the brilliant sapphire blue of the cold, undulating water.

The aromatic coffee did little to lift my spirits. As the ocean watched me, I pored over the job postings, circling those I thought might want me. As I traveled down the rows of job descriptions I began to feel constricted as if physically boxed in. I would break the feeling by looking up and out, westward, to the horizon. It was open and continuous and seemed to stretch, endlessly. I felt expansive when I looked at it. I had stepped into this adventure looking for a feeling of moving beyond whatever boundaries I felt or that life had placed on me, and I now struggled with mental habits of boxing myself in again.

After thumbing through the newspaper, I folded it and headed back to the car. Tomorrow I would make calls and mail resumes. There was nothing more I could do today. The balance of the day stretched ahead of me in an array of possibilities.

I had yet to explore beyond downtown San Diego where the freeway continued on towards Mexico. I headed south on I-5 and after winding through the curves beside the city I noticed the Coronado Bay Bridge stretching across the waters and connecting up to Coronado Island, a *tied-island* at the entrance to San Diego Bay. As if by guided radar, my car curved onto the bridge and traveled over the bay in a graceful arc. Sailboats bobbed in the water beneath the bridge and huge navy ships stood docked in the shipyards. The bridge deposited me in the quaint little village of Coronado and I explored the tree-lined streets of craftsman style houses and tiny shops.

On the ocean side of Coronado, I came upon the crown jewel of the island—The Hotel Del Coronado. I had read about the historic hotel, built in the 1880s with the assistance of Thomas Edison. Old hotels had always intrigued me and this one stood poised on the glistening beach with its red turreted roof and crisp white woodwork. I found a parking spot near the hotel and walked toward the grand lady.

She was all a historic beach resort should be—wood-paneled walls, sheltered courtyard, and a white and red boardwalk where summer travelers danced to live music and ate fragrant snacks sold at the food cabana. The public sections of the hotel were bustling and smelled of the aging Redwood paneling. The energy of 100 years of humanity, luxuriously spending their holidays in the stately building, vibrated in the old hotel.

I wandered down to the gift shop and fingered the expensive trinkets artfully displayed on the shelves. A box tucked towards the back of one shelf caught my eye: clear plastic tubes filled with liquid and glitter. I lifted one of the wands and watched the glitter glisten as it tumbled and floated through the thick, clear fluid. It was almost twelve inches long and as I stood there waving it back and forth I became mesmerized. I looked at the price tag—$10. I was watching every penny I spent now that I had no income, but ten dollars seemed a small price to pay for the lightness I felt watching the swirling, dancing sparkles. I walked to the register, pulled money from my wallet and my tube of magic was placed in a shiny, white gift bag with a rendering of the hotel near the bottom corner. The drawing resembled that of a castle with its cylindrical roof lines and sprawling exterior.

Later that night I sat in Jonathan's apartment by myself. It had been a solitary day, but it had been enjoyable and satisfying. This apartment, unlike the old one in Houston, had a burglar alarm and as I watched its green light blink, I could let go of any residual fear of that night almost a year ago. I sat at the table, my journal next to my *magic wand* from the hotel. I began to write of my experience of suddenly interrupting life, picking up and traveling to a city where I knew no one. Of depositing this loving creature that I had taken into my heart at a temporary holding space while I worked with the process of opening up to whatever might come into my experience. As I wrote, my doubts and fears and hopes and excitement all marched along the page. It had been a daring move for me, the proverbial planner, the Safety-Seeker. I had stepped into the unknown path with only a short lifeline, but it was exhilarating to feel possibilities.

The golden coast of California had held promise to so many in the past, from would-be Gold Rushers to Hollywood stars. Maybe it had something to do with the sparkling ocean, the crispness in the air that had traveled thousands of miles eastward over the Pacific. Maybe it was the energy that percolated up through the fault lines: raw, earth-energy waiting to be transformed into something new. Whatever it was, I was intoxicated with it and I began to open up to whatever good may stretch before me. I grabbed the wand and moved it from side-to-side to watch the glitter tumble and dance and catch the light.

I pretended it was my magic wand and I could wave it around here, now, where I was standing and I could cast a spell that my life would open in new and startling ways. Perhaps it could speak a spell over that voice inside me that whispered of limitations and roadblocks, of fear and doubt, and the spell would silence that voice.

I had been desperately trying to control life and make things happen. But now I was experimenting with stepping into trust and seeing where the flow might take me if I got out of my own way.

I laughed as I sat at the table and waved my enchanted baton, opening the path to whatever possibility or even enchantment might appear on the path before me.

I was glad no one was watching.

Chapter 15

"We must be willing to let go of the life we planned so as to have the life that is waiting for us."
— Joseph Campbell

My path did seem to be magically opening up. I went through the soul-draining motions of job hunting, but reasoned that signing up at a temp agency might be a good interim stage and bring in some much-needed cash. The day after applying, I was dispatched to a job at a financial company located near the 10th hole of the Torrey Pines Golf Course.

"Here," said the woman in the crisp suit and matching heels. "We need to sort through these bags of mail and organize them into piles." Stacks of United Postal Service bags spilled across the conference room floor.

I knew nothing about mortgages or loan servicing but the company was in dire need of warm bodies. The bags of mail, along with truckloads of boxed files, represented the large acquisition the company was urgently trying to sift through. They were desperate for employees and, frankly, I was desperate for a paycheck. The match was made.

I shared an office with another 20-something and our desks both looked out the window to the lush green of the golf course and the mighty blue Pacific beyond. Within three weeks, I was offered a full-time position at a salary that was almost twice what I was making in Houston. Was this serendipity? A lucky streak? It seemed almost too easy.

So things had fallen into place and it looked like I would be staying in San Diego for a bit. As Jonathan's return from his trip approached, I set about looking for a place to live. A conversation with a friend in Houston one night revealed that her old college roommate, Julia, was living in San Diego. She was looking for two roommates. Twenty minutes later I was talking to Julia about the details. We met the next day and she showed me the bedroom that was to be mine. I did not have a stick of furniture, just the clothes I had brought with me, but the rest of the condo was completely furnished. I would be sleeping on the floor for the time being but I was getting used to and having fun with this adventure—of letting go, seeing what presented itself and moving with the tide.

So two months after our caravan had arrived in San Diego, I picked up Jonathan from his world travels and brought him to his little apartment that had offered me shelter for those weeks. We had dinner and he recounted, with great panache, his adventures in Europe, Africa and Asia. I brought Hamlet up to date on my own local happenings (which felt just as adventurous to me) and I left the tired traveler to get some needed sleep as I drove to my new home and my pallet on the floor.

Julia and I hit it off immediately and her optimism and love of laughter were a boon for my still unknown sense of where I was going. Within a few weeks she had found her third roommate and he moved into the bedroom across from mine. Chuck was in his mid-30s, just a few years older than I and the same age as Julia. He was a pilot for TWA and an instructor at Naval Air Station Miramar (NAS Miramar), flight school for F-14 pilots, better known as *Top Gun*. His career and accomplishments were impressive, but he was also kind and wickedly funny.

The three of us settled in to our new living arrangement and cobbled together a kind of family.

My lucky streak continued with a wonderfully comfortable new friendship with a co-worker, Sydney, who had recently moved to San Diego as well, and she took me under her wing and helped me settle in to my new job and environment. Each morning we sat in her office, drank strong, thick coffee and ate butter-laden scones. We laughed and shared stories of our lives. Though I only knew her a short time, our friendship felt familiar and safe. She listened with amusement to the Keisha escapades, stories about her charms and the mayhem. Often, as we would be having our morning talk, I would find a stray Keisha hair in the folds of my clothes. My heart would stop for a moment and I could feel the intense sadness of missing her.

Reports from Keisha's new temporary home came with regularity and were often similar. She continued to push her own boundaries, just as I was pushing mine.

The leash law in my parent's neighborhood posed no real threat to my furry rebel. My parent's property had no fence, so bathroom outings (not on a leash) often led to explorations that went far beyond the yard. Friendship with a poodle down the street (who shared a similar rebel-penchant) had blossomed and seeing her friend poised at the back door some mornings, my mom would let Keisha out for a bit of social time.

It seemed my mom, normally an avid rule-follower, was also testing the bounds of the leash law herself.

Off the two dogs would go to explore whatever might present itself that day. After a couple of hours, Keisha would return solo, with signs of being more than a little tired, but clearly content. On more than one occasion, Keisha's return was heralded by the sound of a Rollinghills police car driving up the steep driveway, Keisha riding shotgun in the passenger seat. Her paws splayed on the dashboard, grinning ear-to-ear, as the dashing officer pulled the car to a stop. My mom would emerge from the house, grateful to see her return. The officer, now a regular at my parent's home, opened the passenger door where Keisha would spring in a happy arc to the ground. As she trotted towards the door, she looked back at the officer as if to say *See ya' tomorrow, Hank*—grateful that the black-and-white-taxi provided door-to-door service.

"Did she get away from you again, Mrs. Tanzer?" the policeman often queried with a smile.

"I'm afraid so," my mom would offer, waving a thanks for returning the delinquent pup.

We would never learn the details of her explorations, but if the contented looks on both her face and the poodle's were any indication, it was more than satisfying.

As I settled into my own routine on the west coast, steady missives from Austin arrived detailing the current state of affairs in the Keisha-Fostering Program. Once my mom had begrudgingly moved past her declaration of not accepting the care of such an errant child, she seemed to enjoy having something to focus on. I suspected Keisha in some way filled the void I had left when I moved out. My mother took great pride in picking out different foods to prepare, buying new replacement rubber pork chops as the old ones were annihilated and, true to my mother's cleanliness obsession, drove Keisha to weekly grooming sessions at the *Bark and Curl*.

My mother's determination in this area sparked and later honed Keisha's equally strong determination to resist anything that had to do with hygiene. The battles were legendary and often ended with my mother pulling Keisha by the leash through the doors of the store, paws spread wide, lips snarling and rear-end planted firmly on the floor. My mother, normally reserved and typically polite, would hunker down and pull with all her might against the strength of Keisha's resistance. It was a fairly matched competition, but always Alice's sheer determination won out and Keisha would emerge two hours later with a bow rubber-banded to her fur and a pout on her snoot.

My dad, similarly, had embraced the new household member and quickly formed his own distinctive relationship with her. She delighted sitting in the passenger seat of his car as she accompanied him on errands. He was an avid walker and now included Keisha on his daily miles-long walks around Town Lake. Being a native Texan, he loved open spaces, so they often went to the off-leash portion of the trail. Yet Keisha rebelled at the last stretch of the walk that returned to the leash rules. Often this ritual ended with the park ranger wagging his fingers at the two and Keisha beginning a game of *catch me* as my dad tried to comply with the ranger's request.

I was scheduled to travel back to Austin for the holidays. I had arranged with my new boss to take a week to spend Christmas with my parents and then drive with Keisha back to San Diego to come live with me, finally.

Two weeks before Christmas I received a letter in the mail with my mother's familiar handwriting on the envelope. The return address was my childhood home but the sender was neither of my parents. It appeared that Keisha was sending an update to the West Coast and my mother had simply been her secretary. The contents were stiff and the size of a postcard.

I eagerly tore open the paper and pulled out a folded card. The cover sported a red Christmas tree and the words: A visit with Santa Paws. Intrigued, I opened the card and a letter spilled from the center. I unfolded the paper and began to read my mother's words. But I quickly learned Keisha had been the author.

"Dear Mom,
I thought the Christmas season was one of joy but that doesn't seem to be the case. Your mother decided to haul me to the pet store last Saturday to have a picture taken with Santa. This was the last thing on my list of weekend fun.
I resisted with every tactic I knew: barking, snarling, trying to run away.
We created quite a stir in the store. The mayhem embarrassed your mom but not enough that she let up on her resolve to pull me into that place and force me, against my better judgement, to sit next to this odd man clad in some get-up.
The crowd of customers seemed to part, like the Red Sea when Moses waved his staff, as your mother and I moved our battle through the center of the store and joined the line for Santa. I grabbed my leash with my mouth and yanked and pulled your surprisingly strong mother in the direction of the door but we only continued our slow march towards the bearded man.
An elf took the leash from your mother and, while I had planted my behind on the floor to try and stop forward movement, shoved me along the concrete floor to the waiting Santa. I

bore down with all my might, growled and bared my teeth. Santa looked alarmed but opened his arms.

It was a blur of arms, legs, paws, beard, growls, and elves with clenched jaws.

But in the end your mother won."

I looked in disbelief at the picture that was framed in the card.

Santa's boots had been splayed in a wide stance to brace himself from the pull to his right. His beard was shifted to the right and his hat fell precariously over one ear. Beads of sweat glistened on his exposed forehead. His glasses, twisted off his nose, rested half-way down his rosy cheeks.

To the left of Santa's throne was Keisha, barely within the frame of the photo, her leash taut with her struggles and Santa's mitten-ed hands grasped the end. Her collar cut into her throat and her tongue spilled out of her mouth as she tussled for escape. A serene landscape of the North Pole offered the backdrop to the battle being played out between St. Nick and a very, very determined dog.

Beneath the picture, the red letters danced in a glittery line: "Merry Christmas!"

The joyous directive and the cheery red glitter were in direct contrast to the scene above. I was at a loss. What in the world was happening back in Austin? I held the picture and note in my hand. My mother was now penning letters as the ghost-writer for Keisha's adventures?

Seems I was not the only one exploring new territory. I looked again at the picture.

Lily Tanzer

I felt great compassion for Santa. He now knew the force of Keisha's will. And, equally, I felt compassion for Keisha. She now knew the force of Alice's will. My parent's mantel held similar postcards of my tiny face contorted in a cry for help and pulling away from a perplexed Santa.

Family traditions continued.

Chapter 16

> *"As you ramble through life, Brother, whatever be your goal, keep your eye upon the doughnut, and not upon the hole."*
>
> — Margaret Atwood,
> The Blind Assassin

Christmas arrived and Keisha and I were finally reunited. It was a joyous and boisterous meeting and we fell in step with each other within moments.

My dad decided to accompany me on the return trip back to California, so the day after Christmas the three of us loaded up the car and headed out for our journey. Keisha was quite comfortable with travel, having made the drive between Houston and Austin many times. My dad had included her on his driving trips to Padre Island where he had grown up and loved to still visit. Those two had made several beach-camping trips to the Gulf Coast. She already seemed to be a seasoned traveler.

Keisha's belongings were again packed into a grocery bag—this time with a few more toys my mother had purchased, including some back-up pork chops—and we stepped onto the same path I had traveled months before.

The weather this time was cold and crisp, the landscape more wind strewn. The drive was monotonous and somewhere in the middle of New Mexico we made another refueling stop. Keisha stayed in the backseat while we both got out to stretch our legs and to fill the tank. My dad had decided to treat himself to a little bag of six powdered donuts from the snack section of the station; food stops were sparse and far-between on the drive. He and I shared the love of stretching a treat out as long as possible and I watched as he ate three of the donuts, meticulously folded the cellophane over the remaining three, and deposited them in the brown paper bag. Crimping the bag shut, he shoved it under his seat for safekeeping. The banker was fastidious in all areas of life—three donuts down, three in savings.

Once the tank was filled, we both walked to the edge of the parking lot and took a moment to look at the vista of desert stretching before us. Keisha, sleeping in the car, was missing the beauty that rolled to the horizon. The mountains in the distance were jagged and purple and offered a crisp delineation between the softness of the cream-colored sand beneath them and the deep blue of the sky above. I breathed in the cool air and was grateful not only for the scenery and the expansiveness but for the companionship of my father and little dog.

Life was good.

Getting back in the car, me behind the wheel and my dad in the front passenger seat, we continued our progress westward. Keisha sat up from her nap in the backseat, cluttered with luggage and her own belongings now being transported to her new home. The miles zoomed by and my dad, feeling a bit peckish, reached beneath his seat and extricated the brown paper bag to finish off his donuts. He peered into the bag and gasped. Pulling out the contents, he held the empty cellophane wrapper in disbelief—only a few powdered sugar crumbs remained. He turned to me in an accusatory way.

"Did you eat my donuts?" he asked with shock and a bit of irritation.

"No!" I answered, confused as to the finding and angry that I was being accused of such a crime. The mood in the car had rocketed swiftly from quiet monotony to acrimony and accusation. My dad took his snacks seriously and I resented being accused of petty theft.

I looked in my rearview mirror at the remaining member of our travel party.

Her dark eyes peered back through the mirror. Nothing changed on her face, but somehow I sensed I might be witnessing my dog's best poker face. No tell-tale crumbs were evident on her muzzle. My dad and I looked at each other in amazement. Then, we both smiled. What deftness must have occurred in the car while we were enjoying the scenery? The stealthy crime had been planned and committed, a crime that seemed a bit improbable.

"Keisha," I said accusingly.

She blinked her dark eyes and stared directly back into mine through the rearview mirror.

I could see the landscape behind her in the back window, scenery that held the memory of some of its famous residents—Jesse James, Billy-the-Kid and The-Hole-in-the-Wall-Gang. These bandits robbed the rumbling stagecoaches and steam-engine trains of their loot, then fled the scene quickly to hide in the vast desert. This criminal snatched her loot, disposed of the evidence and calmly remained at the scene of the crime.

Maybe she was well suited to life in the West.

Finally, Keisha arrived on the West Coast, but with little fanfare. She trotted up the stairs to her new home and like an army officer, surveyed the perimeter of the new barracks and inspected the mess hall as she watched me place her water and food bowl in their new spot. Julia had never lived with a dog before and was more than excited to meet her fourth roommate. They formed a fast friendship and those two often took their own walks together.

Keisha was a social creature and enjoyed her different relationships with everyone. But her relationship with Chuck was truly interesting. I had learned that military aviators are by nature risk takers and somewhat unique. It must take an exceptional personality to command a multi-million dollar machine through the sky at Mach II. His personality was in direct opposition to my own cautious approach but Keisha, as always, found common ground with those around her.

After being gone for days at a time, Chuck would arrive home, usually from his airline run between New York and Paris, and pull treats from his bag for all of us. Trinkets from London and Paris would be doled out to Julia and me and it felt like Christmas each time.

After Julia and I had received our gifts, Chuck, a fan of country western music and a cowboy at heart, ceremoniously donned his black felt cowboy hat and turned his attention to Keisha. A favorite Vince Gill CD was loaded into the stereo and Chuck held out his right hand.

"Shall we?" he asked.

Keisha's tail wagged and she smiled that ear-to-ear grin.

She jumped up towards him, throwing her front paws upward to meet his hands, and balanced on her back paws as the pair began to two-step to the music coming from the speakers. Chuck moved through our living room in time with the music and Keisha followed his lead, not always in time with his steps, but fully engaged in this ritual of theirs. Her charms were many and being Chuck's dance partner held a special place in our household.

We all settled in to the new situation and Keisha adapted easily. Within the span of just over a year she had relocated more times than I had in my whole life. She possessed a resiliency that was admirable, and resourcefulness that served her well, even ferreting out snacks of powdered donuts in the middle of the desert.

Chapter 17

*"I feel the need,
the need for speed."*
— Lt. Pete "Maverick" Mitchell
Top Gun, the movie

Keisha seemed to have quite a bit in common with Chuck and his cadre of aviators. His group of Navy pilots would gather often at our house to watch a football game or just to hang out. Julia and I tended to steer clear of the sometimes-raucous group on those occasions, but Keisha liked being in the thick of things. As the testosterone oozed all over the living room, she seemed to be in her element. She jumped right in with these skilled airmen and participated in the festivities, barking and wagging her tail if voices got a little loud. And I noticed, on the few times I snuck downstairs to grab a snack and peek in on the fun, she seemed especially coquettish. She perked her ears just a tiny bit more and her tail wagged in such a way that the fur on her rump swayed like a hula skirt.

Yes, she fit right in with the bawdy crowd.

She not only enjoyed the attention of these fun-loving guys that seldom allowed a room to be quiet, but she also shared their love of speed and adventure. While Chuck and his friends pushed the limits of gravity from the seat of a 40,000-pound F-14 Tomcat, Keisha was relegated to a smaller, land-bound hunk of steel—my car. I suspected a fighter jet might have been her first choice, but my little sports car offered a good alternative.

I needed only to ask, "Keisha, would you like to go for a ride?" and her ritualistic dance of delight commenced, first witnessed on the beach in Galveston, circling several times before standing and wagging her tail furiously from side to side. *Eeps* and *peeps* emanated from her throat and her tail would swish furiously, making her back paws alternately leave the ground.

She would jump into the passenger seat with the ferocity of a lunging tiger and thrust her face to the window, urging it to open. I would comply and push the electronics so that she was able to extend, almost full body, out the window and into the oncoming rush of air. The look on Keisha's face as she soaked in the sights, sounds and smells of our journey was the best illustration of bliss that I had ever seen.

Chuck and his crew pushed the forces of gravity and so did she. She leaned as far out of the window as possible, seeming to find that edge where the laws of physics take over and she might topple to the road—the *Danger Zone*.

As her front paws gripped the door as a cantilever to extend her upper body as far into the wind/rain/sunshine as possible, her ears peeled back against the wind, her eyes squinted and her mouth opened to bite and snap at the rushing air.

An occasional snapping at passing road signs was the only clue that she was processing anything other than the intense sensations of the wind through her fur. She rode the Danger Zone like a surfer rides a twenty-foot wave.

Her enjoyment usually entertained other drivers and I often waved back at the thumbs-up or applause coming our way.

There was no doubt she concurred with the eloquent words of John Gilliespie Magee, Jr.

Oh! I have slipped the surly bonds of earth
And danced the skies on laughter-silvered wings.

To be near this experience of rapture, even tangentially, was exhilarating and I found myself enjoying her trips in the car almost as much as she did. I marveled in the pleasure that such a mundane experience could bring. And I began to notice other dogs on the road, being chauffeured to and fro, having their own experience. So as Keisha played with the onslaught of rushing air, I became a bit of a zoologist, a Dian Fossey-of-the-roadways. Not *Gorillas in the Mist*, but perhaps *Dogs on the Highway*. It was fascinating to see how differently each dog took to the streets, unique to their own personality. And as in most fields of research, patterns of behavior began to emerge, behavior that communicates a lot about the individual and his approach to life.

My research revealed five main categories.

The first: *The total immersion of the senses and/or the thrill-seeker*. (Keisha was included in this category). Usually as much of the body as possible was involved and therefore included seemingly dangerous contortions out the window. Faster speeds were preferred as they created the best wind experience coupled with a lottery of smells. Especially lucky days were those with some inclement weather—fog, rain or snow. At times the ecstasy became so consuming that one pushed past safety at risk of flying out the window, although Keisha saw nothing wrong with that. Companions needed to be vigilant in watching for these critical moments.

Knowing that fighter pilots had their call signs stenciled on the plane beneath the canopy of their jet, I thought it might not be a bad idea to include something similar for this group stenciled on their own door.

A second group might have been labeled: *"I enjoy the passing scenery of life from my comfortable seat"* group. This group, too, acknowledged the pleasure of moving through space with a window to the world but saw no reason why any physical energy should have been expended. For smaller breeds, this entailed hoisting front paws to the door for better viewing, but short breaks were needed to rest. For those blessed to have been a large enough breed to remain being seated—all the better!

A third group emerged as the more pragmatic: *"We are Busy Getting to our Destination"* group. No fuss, no muss. Eyes on the road. Side windows offered only distractions. Keep the eyes straight ahead. These dogs preferred the co-pilot, front-seat position. Once stopped at traffic behind a tiny European car, I witnessed a large Bouvier, perched in the middle of the back seat, as the front seat was taken by a human. The dog and his companions sat patiently at the intersection during rush hour while streams of cross traffic flowed in front of their car. The occupants stared forward and shared a subtle, synchronous back-and-forth movement with the traffic, as if watching a tennis match. The dog's massive curly head moved in time with his companions.

Additionally, a fourth group formed: the *"ADD/ADHD"* or *"Someone Put Sugar in my Kibbles"* group. A rarer breed that could be difficult to watch without inducing motion sickness. These dogs moved rapidly about between the front seat, the back seat, over to one side, back to the other. *Look at the back window, look out the side, check the driver to make sure they are focusing—'cause I'm not.* Frenetic at times, anxious mostly. Perhaps the movement of the car was stimulating with all the new sights and sounds or there was anticipation about the destination. Or maybe there was just really good, paw-tapping oldies playing on the radio. Either way, the nervous system was in high gear. An occasional pat or hug could calm for a brief second but the laws of inertia were at work.

Finally, the last and least energetic of the bunch: the elusive *"A Car Ride=A Nap"* group. Elusive because the reclined position of the nap made it virtually impossible to spot this group from another car. Occasionally one glimpsed a tousled head poke itself up for a quick survey of the landscape but generally these were a stealthy bunch. I suspected their motto might have been *Wake me up when we get there.*

Dogs and their companions shuttling here and there, getting to wherever they were going, it was quite a business of transportation and variety of nature. With Keisha though, the journey *was* the destination. And as usual, we were often a study in contrasts. I held no love of journeys, rather I just wanted to get there and lie down. At times she would extricate herself from the wind and the pleasure and step toward me with her fur in a wild halo around her head. Her eyes would dance and she turned her head a bit as she questioned me: *are you getting it?*

I couldn't be sure exactly what she was asking me but I think the answer was probably *no.*

Chapter 18

"A family has its own rituals and its own superstitions."
— Tea Obreht

Life on Trieste Lane was rich in rituals. We had formed a motley family of sorts, each with our own idiosyncrasies and preferences. The fact that we all liked each other allowed us to make room for and at times even participate in some of the routines we honed throughout our lives. Keisha was no different.

Her evening dining ritual had emerged shortly after she arrived. Each night, she delicately sampled her food from the bowl. After a moment or two, she began tucking the small bits of kibble gingerly in her mouth, carrying them, like an altar boy carrying the Eucharist, to the open space of our living room. There she would deposit each kibble, plopping them one-by-one in some pattern of which only she knew the significance. It required several trips until just the right amount of bits were arranged across the floor. Upon completion, she would plop her rump down next to the mysterious arrangement and look, with piercing eyes, at each of us. The look was so penetrating that we felt disarmed, sitting on the couch, observing the somber ceremony. This sparked much speculation.

"Do you think she's showing us the structure of the universe?" queried Julia one evening, with a hint of seriousness. That's one of the things I loved about Julia; she thought so highly of Keisha that she was willing to entertain the idea of my dog being tapped into some cosmic configuration.

I looked at the grainy pellets, some placed closely to one another and others sat far away from the clusters of the rest.

"Maybe it's some form of hieroglyphics with ancient hidden wisdom," I joked back.

Sarcasm aside, this was all more than a little odd.

Keisha continued her penetrating gaze aimed at us both, the kibbles lying silently between us, withholding their cryptic message. I was beginning to feel a bit like Indiana Jones, scratching his head over some nebulous missive.

"Maybe it's a critique of the quality of dog food in America," offered Chuck from the kitchen.

Keisha didn't seem bothered by our inability to decipher her kibble-code. After a few moments of watching us scan the canine version of a crop circle laid out on the carpet, she headed back to the kitchen where the loud sound of crunching could be heard as she polished off the remainder of her dinner. Her appetite sated, she headed back to living room, splayed onto her belly and nestled her snoot onto her front paws with a sigh. From this vantage point, she surveyed her work for a second time. After some minutes she stood up and ambled to each bit, delicately consuming it, before moving to the next one. The message was now erased from the world.

The scenario played out each evening, without any of us ever decoding whatever communication she was skillfully crafting with those brown pellets of food.

Other rituals were less perplexing and more prone to being savored.

Julia reserved each Sunday for a true day of sloth. She emerged downstairs, in her oversized terry robe well after the noon hour. She nested in the corner of our L-shaped couch, gathered the Sunday paper and cradled a steaming cup of coffee while she consumed in well-planned order—comics, Life&Style, Entertainment, local then national news, and finally the Editorials.

Somewhere between local and national news, hunger pangs would set in and a snack was warranted. Having worked for years in restaurants, she assembled her food with great care and presentation. Carrying it back to the couch, she nibbled it, leisurely, while finishing up the paper. A nap followed shortly thereafter.

Keisha enjoyed Julia's finely tuned schedule and often joined her on the couch, curled up just beyond Julia's feet. By the time Julia set the whole thing in motion, we had been down to the beach for a walk, eaten breakfast and Keisha had been busy monitoring the neighborhood comings and goings through the windows.

One wintery Sunday with rain falling relentlessly against the windows, Julia and Keisha lounged in their usual spots when Julia, having forged through most of the paper already, remembered the box of leftover spaghetti from her date the previous night. Keisha remained in her snoot-to-tail position while the clatter of food preparation emanated from the kitchen. Julia rounded the corner carrying a steaming plate of pasta and a can of cola. Keisha's black eyes tracked Julia's every move as the food was placed carefully on the glass coffee table and the pillows and blankets were fluffed and rearranged for the culinary portion of the afternoon.

"Forgot the parmesan," Julia muttered under her breath as she quickly walked back into the kitchen. Keisha's tranquil eyes continued to follow her movements.

Moments later, Julia returned, settled back into the couch cushions and reached for the pasta. The white porcelain of the bowl glistened. Not a trace of the rich tomato sauce or strands of spaghetti remained. Stunned, Julia turned to Keisha, still curled in her original position at the end of the couch. Her tail wrapped over her nose, so that her eyes peered out from atop the fur, much like a bandit peering from beneath his scarf. Julia turned back to the empty bowl and shook her head. Less than two minutes had elapsed during the cheese retrieval. She turned back to Keisha, still snuggled in her own nest, not a hair out of place, not a sign of mischief. The dark eyes calmly stared back with innocence and concern as to what possibly could have transpired in those brief moments. There appeared to be no witness to the crime.

Julia, still incredulous, carried the bowl back to the kitchen and was resigned to forage for something else. Back on the couch, Keisha let out a satisfied sigh and, tummy full, closed her eyes to enjoy a post-lunch nap.

Chapter 19

"Of all the things you choose in life, you don't get to choose what your nightmares are. You don't pick them. They pick you."
— John Irving

My bold experiment on the West Coast was nearing its second year. Life at our condo was entertaining, happy and nourished me, but I felt increasingly alone in the romance department. I went out on dates, but I didn't seem to connect with anyone.

Keisha was proving to be an accurate barometer of my potential partners. She would initially sniff each suitor and interact with them for the first thirty minutes or so, but after a bit she would reach some sort of conclusion and saunter to her favorite green chair where she would sit, snoot-to-tail, and wait until I had come to her same conclusion: *nope, not this one.*

Life had fallen into place with such ease since my move, but this area of my life remained unfulfilled. I was not lonely. My life was full. But something was missing. Keisha had begun to heal those parts deep inside me that had initially been opened but then shut down after those seven long years with *him*. It was not a new relationship with a man that had begun to transition the trauma and battening down of my heart, but instead my little dog had initiated the shift. I had invited her into my life for protection at a time when my vulnerability was at a new high. But she was proving to be anything but a great protector. In fact, I suspected her social nature might have directed a would-be burglar to the location of anything of value in my home. Instead, she was stepping into my life through some odd side door. Her very being was softening parts of me that had, unknowingly, been guarded and focused on priorities that were not my own.

I tried to relax into the contentment that existed and to stop focusing on plans for the future.

I was stronger, less guarded and it was with reluctance that I agreed to a blind date with the brother of a co-worker, not long after my 29th birthday.

"I think you guys would hit it off," my friend said, smiling.

I had heard those words before.

But this time they proved to be accurate.

We did *hit it off*. The conversation was easy, comfortable and the tiniest hint of a spark ignited the evening. There had been high voltage with *him* all those years. A tiny spark may be safer, I thought.

Dave was 18 months younger than I and had recently moved to Southern California from Minnesota where he had grown up. He possessed All-American good looks, a keen intelligence and a gentle spirit. We shared our experiences of moving to San Diego and how different it felt from our childhood homes—foreigners in a new land. He was thoughtful, not just kind, but a deep thinker. A few years earlier his mother had divorced his father and left their life in the rural area where he had grown up to move to Hawaii. The breakup of his family had clearly affected him, and he sought stability and comfort, two aspects of life on my list as well.

On several of his mother's visits to see Dave, she sat with us as we shared steaming cups of coffee brewed from the Kona beans she hand-delivered, and we journeyed with her through her stories of the gentle, lush landscapes of the islands. She told us what she had learned about the concepts of harmony within the Huna beliefs and the miraculous healing powers of forgiveness and reconciliation of the practice of Ho'oponopono. I had been to Hawaii before, but I had only cavorted with the touristy aspects. I had not met the deeper layer of the islands. I was intrigued and wanted to know more.

A sports fanatic, Dave's interests also ran eclectic and deep. Earlier, he had introduced me to Celtic Runes and taught me to use the stones, with their tiny images of an ancient alphabet stenciled on their faces, to divine answers to questions or to explore meanings behind events. I had never used such tools and they reminded me a bit of the Rorschach images from my psychology classes. While I was not sure the stones held magical or mystical messages, I was intrigued by the process of extrapolating the stone's message to fit within the context of the subject or question it was chosen to address. Often the stone's meaning was instantly apparent to the situation, but other times the mind needed to search and explore before a connection could be discerned.

It felt good to be in a relationship again, and Dave was unlike anyone I had ever met. I felt safe and did not fear the deception and guardedness that had so permeated my previous relationship, and our connection grew quickly.

Almost too quickly.

But I was so happy to have found someone so gentle and kind, and I allowed the pace of our relationship to move faster than felt comfortable. The heart's desires are strong but often stubbornly cloud our judgment.

My mom visited a few months after we met and the three of us laughed and played together. He seemed to be joining the family. And yet as Dave and I spent more time together, a recurring dream that I had had for years, starting about the age of 14, resurfaced and visited me often in the middle of the night. Each dream had its own unique particulars but it was all the same general scenario.

It was my wedding day. I was either donning my wedding dress amidst the bridesmaids, driving to the church, or the denouement---walking down the aisle. In all of those scenarios, I was panicked, adrenaline surged through my veins and I wanted, no *needed*, to flee the ceremony and the faceless groom standing at the altar. The dream often played out like an action-packed movie, with the theme from Mission Impossible playing in the background. I always awoke sweating and heart pounding. It was life or death. These nightmares often came during those seven years with *him,* but had been dormant the last couple years. Now they returned with a vengeance.

As Dave and I sat in the evenings together, he reading the paper or a book and me playing with Keisha, I would often watch him and I could feel the terror and determination of the dreams move into the room with us. I would shake off the feeling and pray that the dreams would leave me and my new relationship alone.

But changes were afoot in our household.

Chuck had surprised us all and fallen quickly, hopelessly in love and now was moving on from our happy little condo to make a new life with his bride. We needed a third roommate to make the rent manageable, so after some consideration and discussion with Julia, it was decided that Dave would now become our new roommate.

He would be a perfect addition to the household and we all gathered around the TV each night with Julia for her ritual *Jeopardy* watching and Keisha, again, had found common ground with whomever life presented. She often went with Dave on his runs through the local park or outings to get doughnuts on Saturday mornings or watched football games blasting from the TV with her new friend and roommate. Dave was enamored with my best friend. Few could escape her charms.

On the surface it seemed a good and logical choice.

But the dreams continued.

Chapter 20

"Unexpected events can set you back or set you up. It's all a matter of perspective."
— Mary Anne Radmacher

Not only were my dreams robbing me of sleep, worries at work were making my nights restless as well. Rumors were flying that several contracts were not being renewed and that significant downsizing loomed on the horizon. My department would be an area of major upheaval.

I proactively updated my resume with my newfound experience and cast a net for potential positions in the area. Each inquiry was answered with polite letters stating they had no openings at the time. But a new position in my personal life was opening up: Dave had begun to talk about marriage. At first I was excited, despite the dreams lurking in my nights. A happy marriage and, more importantly, children was at the top of my list of life goals. The last few years I had quietly let them lie dormant while I dealt with what life served up. He urged me to go ring shopping yet I never failed to find an excuse. He began to grow weary of asking and was rightfully upset that I seemed so hesitant. We argued more and enjoyed each other less.

Nevertheless, we packed our car early that January, with Keisha in the backseat, and drove east to Texas to celebrate Anna's wedding. Keisha was going along so that she might visit her old friend, Chandon. The reunion was as expected. Keisha eagerly vaulted to Chandon's side while he stoically braced for the onslaught of her affections.

Things had not changed much since Keisha had become a Californian.

The wedding was an elegant and beautiful affair with Anna and her husband often casting a twinkling eye at Dave and me, hinting that we were next. A knot grew in my stomach as Dave looked at me with hope and a little bit of fear. I had been battling a flu for weeks and the symptoms ebbed and flowed. By the time we headed home to California my fever was well over 102 degrees and my chest ached when I breathed.

We walked back into our life on the West Coast with a visceral distance between us, and I headed for the doctor. Antibiotics were prescribed for the pneumonia that was now diagnosed, and I crawled into bed and waited to feel better. But relief never seemed to come. After a few weeks, my chest stopped feeling like a heavy stone pushed against it, but nausea had replaced it. The churning of my stomach made food repellant to me and brought a heavy feeling of anxiety to my day. I couldn't sleep, even on the nights where the dream stayed away. I felt shaky and weak. Headaches plagued me at every turn. I had returned to work, which was still rife with layoff rumors. The Christmas tree still sat in the corner as January turned to February. It was dry and brittle and the ornaments that had looked so festive during the holidays took on a dull sheen. Life was slogging forward with no real momentum.

Visits to doctors yielded no answers to my intensifying symptoms and I was beginning to panic about what might happen. I couldn't afford to continue to burn through my sick leave like I was. I had been transferred to a new department as a response to the turmoil in the company. I did not like the work I was doing and my added physical illness made my days feel hopeless. It was a vicious cycle—worrying about not being well enough to return to work intensified the churning in my stomach and continued the insomnia.

One afternoon in mid-February, while driving east along the freeway to get back to work after a doctor appointment, I noticed in my periphery a car merging onto the freeway at an alarming speed. Before I could process what happened, the car careened across three lanes and slammed into mine. The collision of the two speeding cars climaxed in an instant, but stretched in a warped, slow motion blow.

The sickening sound of metal crunching, of glass shattering filled my ears as our two cars made contact and skidded to their resting places, on the grassy embankment of the highway divider. When the motion stopped, I sat motionless too, gripping my steering wheel and seeing the shattered glass of my windshield strewn across the dashboard.

I was still alive.

The car that had hit me skidded to a halt and sat motionless at a 45 degree angle from my own. A man emerged from the car. He was alive too. My engine was quiet while the cars whizzed by, and several pulled over to help. Blood dripped from my forehead, my hands were shaking. My head hurt. My fingers picked bits of my windshield from my hair. I opened my door and walked toward a woman who had pulled over to help. I took a breath and my lungs filled with air. She walked toward me, grabbed my hands and led me, zombie-like, back to her car. It was an odd refuge among the turbulent wind flowing in both directions of the freeway.

Within moments, a police car joined the spectacle, along with an ambulance. The stranger who had slammed into my life kept his distance from me and offered no eye contact. We each spent time in the ambulance being checked for serious injuries by the EMS technician. Cuts were bandaged and we both were deemed relatively okay.

"You'll be sore tomorrow," the paramedic said. "But nothing seems to be serious. You'll be okay." He patted my leg to emphasize the point.

I wished I could have believed him.

The paperwork was filled out by the police officer, insurance information exchanged with the other driver, the tow truck carried away the crippled cars and the business end of the highway transaction was completed. The Good Samaritan, who had walked me to her car for refuge, drove me the short distance home.

It was mid-afternoon and the condo was quiet as Julia and Dave were at work.

But Keisha was waiting.

Clocks were not part of her life, so the timing of my return did not seem out of place to her. I was still shaking from the experience and collapsed onto the couch to try and sort through the events. She leapt onto the cushion beside me and I grabbed the sides of her face, planting a long, hard kiss on her forehead. Tiny pieces of windshield glass fell onto her fur.

I was alive.

My life felt like a mess, but I was here.

Keisha wagged her tail in agreement.

Chapter 21

"Don't tell me the moon is shining; show me the glint of light on broken glass."
— Anton Chekhov

The ambulance tech's words were prophetic. The next day at work I was so sore that I could barely reach for the ringing desk phone.

Eventually, I picked it up.

"Lily Tanzer," I announced, not sure I was very happy to be her.

It was Dave.

"I've got some news," he said, excitement in his voice. It was good to hear the soft timbre. It had been comforting last night as he consoled me after the accident and it was just as comforting now.

"I've been talking to Dan, my old boss at the bank in Minneapolis. A trader position has opened up and he's offered it to me."

The car yesterday had come quickly from the on ramp to my right but this came from left field and completely blind-sided me. Two hits in less than twenty-four hours.

"Oh," I said, inadequately. I knew that Dave had always wanted that position. I sat in my cubicle, sore, nauseated, and still shaking a bit, and listened to the future that Dave now was looking to.

His words finally wound down, and he waited for my response.

"Wow. This is a lot to take in. Let's talk about it tonight," I said. That was about all I could muster as I eyed the files on my desk, eavesdropping on my conversation and waiting to be dealt with.

As I backed away from the conversation, I placed the phone in its cradle. A dull ache burned down my arm. I looked again at the light blue, legal-sized file folders thick with paper, scattered on my desk. There was so much to do and I couldn't think. My body ached but my mind seemed numb.

The physical discomfort, coupled with my mental overwhelm, gave me but a few options. I walked into my boss's office and said I was leaving early. He was concerned about me, especially after the events of yesterday, and he stood up from his chair, walked towards me and put his arm around me gently, knowing that every part of me hurt.

"Of course," he said. He walked me out of his office and watched me grab my purse. I knew he was concerned about me, but I was also aware he was concerned about the unattended files on my desk.

That night, Dave and I gathered on the couch. No *Jeopardy* tonight. Julia had retreated to her bedroom. Keisha snoozed under the coffee table. I felt like joining her, but my body ached too much.

"Nothing will change between us," he offered. "We'll just have a long distance relationship. I'll travel to San Diego often and you can come north. Maybe eventually move with me." His eyes seemed truthful about his plans for the future. But my feelings of betrayal were real, too. Betrayal and I had met before. Too often, it seemed. It was delivered to me frequently from *him*, but I had served it up as well so I wasn't only a victim.

I felt too awful physically to say much. My stomach roiled and my gut knew that he had taken the job to put distance between us, even if he wasn't aware of it. And I couldn't blame him. I leaned back on the couch cushion and gingerly placed my head against the soft fabric. I could feel a tiny splinter of windshield push into my scalp. It would take weeks before I stopped finding shattered glass in my hair.

Parts of me were numb but others were not.

Dave spent the rest of the evening making calls and working on the logistics of his move. He couldn't waste any time; his new job started in two weeks. I spent the rest of the evening on the couch with Keisha snoozing in the crook of my legs. She seemed unconcerned with all that had transpired. Life was good for her. She was where she wanted to be. And that seemed to be nestled on the couch with me.

Dave was excited about his future.

Keisha was content with her present.

Discomfort and fear marked my present and future. I was feeling boxed in again. And I couldn't see the horizon.

Chapter 22

"To accomplish great things we must not only act, but also dream; not only plan but also believe."
— Anatole France

The next week, my walks with Keisha were slow, often painful, and longer than usual only because of my inability to walk quickly. But we covered a lot of metaphorical ground and I thought I had found the horizon point.

I finally reached the conclusion that I needed to stop the current treadmill and see if I could get my health back. I had no vacation or sick-leave hours left, but calculations concluded that I had enough money in the bank for a one-month leave of absence from work, to try and get things back on track. I was not unhappy to let my boss know that I would be gone for four weeks. He was well aware that I was not healthy (or happy). With great fear, I walked away from my office and my paycheck and circled up to try and right my course.

While I walked away from my work to heal, Dave was turning toward a new job and new home. Keisha and I waved goodbye early one Saturday morning as Dave's car pulled out of the driveway and headed north. My dog and I headed back inside and I crawled into bed to begin my allotted time to get my body well again. I pulled the blanket over me and Keisha burrowed under, finding the edge of my body and nudging against me as she found her place.

I looked at the calendar hanging next to the window, where morning sun flowed through the blinds—30 days to right myself.

I sighed and closed my eyes.

If I wasn't well enough to return to work in that time, would I need to move back to Texas? Finances might dictate that. I loved my parents and I knew they would welcome me. But that seemed like a huge step backward.

I had good friends in Texas, a history in Texas. But that history was not all good. Returning to familiar things might not be all comforting and positive. Maybe I could move to be with Dave and his new life. The thought of the snowy winters made me shiver, and the cold I felt didn't come entirely from the weather. Everything that had to do with Dave seemed uncertain. I closed my eyes and tried to feel, discern, despite the nausea, what my gut was saying.

My time in California didn't seem fulfilled yet.

But I could not see beyond those 30 days.

As I approached my thirtieth birthday, I was standing in another uncomfortable "present." My past was tapping me on the shoulder many nights in my dreams, and my future was unclear and didn't seem easy.

Over the course of my month away from work, Keisha and I spent 24 hours a day together. She slept beside me as I researched my symptoms and forged new, healthy diet plans. I had no energy, but she urged me to get outside. She would bring her red leash and deposit it on the bed.

"Let's get some air," her eyes urged.

We took gentle walks through the park and beside the ocean. I let go of my fast, driven pace of walking and timing myself, normally measuring my progress along the trail. I couldn't do that at this point even if I tried. We stopped frequently on our walks to sit and listen to the sounds around us. The California sun was warm and nourishing. I soaked up the rays and drank in the solitude and quiet with Keisha. And I sent a prayer to my future, whatever and wherever that was.

I watched the balance of my checking account deplete as fear and doubt crept in.

I had closed my account at the bank where my father worked and opened a new one in California months ago. Neither Dad nor Herb could monitor the health of this account. Nor could they call me with assistance. The old account was often depleted by Keisha's vet visits. The California account was now being depleted by my own medical issues.

Twenty more days.

I inhabited the *Health* aisles of the bookstore, searching for answers to my discomfort. I gave up caffeine, sugar, wheat and yeast. Oh, the pain of sitting on the couch watching Julia and Keisha partake of a bag of donuts, hot and glistening with a sticky glaze. Keisha smacked and gulped the yeasty dough and Julia dipped hers into a steaming cup of coffee. What friends!

Change was hard.

But I soon was spending most of my time at the bookstore in the metaphysical section. Testing the concept of letting go of the old, and tempting the fates in my California move had proved fruitful. Now I was looking beyond just letting go. I was sculpting the next step, the next manifestations. The letting go part was effective but more passive. All these books urged a more engaged role in shaping the future. The notion that we were creators of our life and that we shaped the very course of our path with our intentions and thoughts brought a new energy into my body. It was a relatively new concept to me. I was used to forging ahead with action and willpower, but I couldn't muster much of either at this point. The concept that thoughts and intentions could actually churn the ether and influence the future was an intriguing one. Could thoughts and intentions really be as powerful as actions? I had little to lose, I thought. It stirred hope in me and resonated with a truth buried somewhere deep inside.

During those quiet days alone with Keisha, I decided to revisit my love of drawing. I rummaged through a closet and found an old sketchpad. There was something richly satisfying in moving my pencil along the crisp, white paper and directing the lines and shadings in different patterns. Soon a picture, a scene, a vignette or scribbles even, was born—something that had not existed before.

I splurged on a small box of pastel chalks. The powdery sticks allowed me to move color onto the page, some vibrant and bold, others soft and feathery. Keisha lounged beside me and often was in the line of fire as I blew the excess pastel dust from my drawing. Pinks, purples, greens nestled in her black fur. It was all part of our creative process. I only had enough energy to move the chalk across the paper, but I was still creating.

Fifteen more days.

I went to the library and checked out books on nutrition, healing and those authors from the metaphysical section I had been drawn to at the bookstore. Dave called frequently with updates and reminded me of the authors his mom had recommended. Keisha and I spent our days moving quietly through the condo while Julia was at work. But we were not alone. Shakti Gawain, Napoleon Hill, Wayne Dyer, and Deepak Chopra all joined us and urged us on a new path.

"Create with your thoughts," they cheered.
The student lounged in bed amidst the blankets, pillows and furry dog while herbal tea steeped on the bedside stand for our daily work.

Julia, Keisha and I gathered on the couch at night for *Jeopardy* and Julia offered a compassionate and supportive ear to my worries.

More books and more teachers gathered in the bed with us. Emmet Fox, Maxwell Maltz, and Norman Vincent Peale. Catherine Ponder coaxed me to pull out pad and paper and begin to formulate what

I wanted to manifest in my life—to move from the broad to the specific. The books urged me to look beyond what my rational mind thought was possible. I thought back to my art teacher's explanation of how the rational mind could prevent us from seeing things clearly.

So I pulled out my sketchpad and turned to a fresh, blank page. I put pen to paper and began to list the things I wanted in my life: health, rewarding work, happiness. While I had done similar exercises before, this time I was told to be specific. To lay out time (oh, I loved to do that already) and then detail exactly what I would like to manifest. *Be specific*, these teachers prodded me. I was timid at first, aware that reality must be watching my plans.

Fear loomed over my bed as I explored my heart's desires. And wrote.

This daughter of a banker first wrote conservatively, things that the Universe might be willing to dole out in the current situation. But soon I let go of some of those internal and external restrictions and played with bigger possibilities. The horizon broadened.

As I changed my diet and exercised daily in a slow and purposeful way, I watched the balance of my bank account tick down. I watched the calendar and saw, staring at me, the projected date of my return to work. I had planned that date around the number in my savings account. Reality was about limited resources, wasn't it?

The fear was creeping into my being, but every time I felt it rise in a wave through my core, I pulled out my paper and pen and focused that energy into planning what my future *could* hold.

Ten more days.

Keisha snuggled beside me, snoring lightly, as I boldly wrote my three-month, six-month, one-year and five-year desires. I looked at what I had written and my logical mind sneered. *No way in hell could that happen.* But I noticed it also gave me a sense of hope and excitement that shifted my feelings of illness and dis-ease. I had forgotten about my magic wand from the Hotel Del Coronado, but it reminded me how I had actually done something similar when I journaled my move to California. I had used the wand as a talisman for my power to create the trajectory of my life.

But now I was not just opening my mind to possibilities, I was focusing my thought into creating, shaping, sculpting the future. My logical mind scoffed but something deeper embraced the process.

Five more days.

I wrote bold statements about income, work, happy relationships and, most tangibly, a seaside home. Dare I be able to live beside that beautiful, undulating sea of blue? Now, we needed to drive ten minutes for Keisha and me to be there—the beach offering a welcome path for our walks. But I longed to see it from my windows, to hear it from my bed, to smell it from my patio. Wasn't I lucky enough to be that close already?

It seemed selfish but it's what I longed for.

Still feeling nauseated and weak, I tucked my list of future events into a drawer and moved reluctantly toward the date of returning to work. In those short thirty days, I had changed my diet, my schedule, the way I moved and more importantly I began to change my thoughts and my mental habits.

One more day.

I had always loved *before and after* photos. I loved the dramatic juxtaposition of the undesired, the unorganized, and the unwanted morphed magically into the beautiful, elegant, organized result. The ugly duckling, magically, mystically, became the graceful swan. It was delicious and I couldn't ever seem to get enough. But I knew that what stretched between those two snapshots of time was a process, a process of change that could be messy, slow and fraught with missteps. I also knew that the *after* picture was merely a snapshot in time. The elegance, the beauty, the organization, the health would change too and move to another picture. And so the process of life goes.

Happily ever after was not the end of the story.

No more days.

Now, three days before my thirtieth birthday, one of those milestone events, I stepped back into my office and my work feeling only mildly better. I missed my hourly connection to Keisha. I wasn't sure my self-imposed respite had been a success. I still felt unwell. I was put on a new project and moved forward without any hint of how I might work my way out of this feeling of dissatisfaction and unease. But the seeds of hope had been planted, and I was aware of something germinating. It felt like the universal forces had been sitting beside me and my writing, on my sculpting of the ethers and had recognized my efforts at releasing the fears and doubts.

Coming home for lunch several weeks after my return to work, I was greeted by my answering machine blinking with a message from a company to whom I had sent my resume months earlier. The woman's voice was crisp and professional: they wanted to interview me for a position that fit the one I had to leave behind at my current company. I still wasn't feeling well and doubted whether I was up to changing jobs, but I picked up the phone and made a date for the interview.

Three weeks later I was at my new job, at a salary that matched exactly the amount I had written on my three-month plan. And I had received a signing bonus that replenished my depleted bank account.

I had turned a corner.

But my path still seemed unclear.

Chapter 23

"Beginnings are sudden, but also insidious. They creep up on you sideways, they keep to the shadows, they lurk unrecognized. Then, later, they spring."
— Margaret Atwood
The Blind Assassin

My new job brought a whole new cast of characters, and I slipped right into the group. The new company provided a completely different atmosphere from my old one. It was relaxed, less formal. Many mornings the table outside my boss's office was laden with bags of bagels, an array of cream cheeses, donuts, and pastries all deposited there by my coworkers. They seemed to be in on the knowledge that productivity is fueled by simple carbohydrates and saturated fat. They were more than happy to pitch in for the common good.

Not only did this company have a "casual Friday" dress code, we enjoyed "casual Monday" attire as well. My brain worked better when my feet weren't bound up in hose and heels. My blue jeans allowed me to move better in my little cubicle and to think more clearly as I tapped away at my computer. And while the work was just as demanding and intense, the undercurrent that flowed between the departments and between the employees did not hold some of the contentious atmosphere from my previous employer. Many of my coworkers felt like old friends even though I had known them only a short while. I breathed easier as I settled into my new space, and I was amazed at how much I enjoyed going to work.

My health continued its steady pace forward and Julia and I now spent nights and weekends looking for a new place to live. Without Dave's share of the rent, we decided to downsize.

Julia called me at work one morning, breathless and excited.

"Remember my friend Myra? Well, her ex-husband's old girlfriend's ex-college roommate...." Julia' vast social network often sent conversations winding around and down this very path. I held on for the final curve and then we'd be moving forward again. "...knows this couple who are moving to a big house on Mt. Soledad." There, I think we were on the straightaway finally. "They need to rent out their condo near Wind and Sea beach and haven't been able to find anyone they can trust. They basically want some trustworthy people they know to live in it, with minimal rent, until they can sell it."

Well, we didn't qualify for all of the categories, but we were trustworthy and I was hoping minimal rent fell into our definition.

That night we met the four-degrees-of-separation-couple at the soon-to-be-vacant condo. Julia and I both shared furtive glances at each other as we took in the 180-degree ocean view and tried to hold our excitement from spewing all over the cream-colored carpets. It was amazing.

We chatted with the couple and learned that they ultimately wanted to sell the property, but the real estate market was severely depressed and that was proving difficult. They quoted the rent, completely within our budget, but in return for the reduced rent we would be allowing potential buyers to view the property while we lived there. And they could only offer a month-to-month lease. Julia and I shared a glance. No problem.

It all seemed too good to be true. There was one fly in the ointment. We had left our third roommate behind and it was unclear if the owners might allow a dog into this beautiful environment. I eyed the carpet with a fair amount of trepidation.

"Lily has a little dog." Julia boldly forged ahead. "She's very well behaved." Julia clearly stretched the truth more than a bit. We both watched our potential landlord's faces with our breath held.

"No problem," the wife said. "I love dogs! Can I meet her?"

"Of course," Julia cheered, clapping her hands together. We both smiled and looked at each other. "You've never met another dog like her."

Now Julia was being more truthful.

So within weeks after ending my nauseous and fearful thirty day leave-of-absence, I was in a new, well-paying job, feeling stronger and healthier and now I was living, with my dear friends Julia and Keisha, in our luxurious condo, overlooking the Pacific Ocean. I thought about my little apartment on Lake Street and the shaggy brown carpet.

We'd come a long way, Keisha.

Dave had come to visit several times since his move, but was often anxious to get back to the job he clearly loved. I didn't mind the long-distance relationship at all. I had so much in my life now that Dave's physical presence didn't seem necessary. I was hoping, too, that the miles would somehow allow a quicker resolution of the issues that sat between us.

The nightmares had lessened, too.

Later that August, we planned a celebration for Julia's birthday. My company was hosting the Summer Pops by the Bay, and Tchaikovsky was slated for the Thursday night of Julia's celebration. She and I coordinated a group of friends for a picnic and music.

Julia had invited James, whom she had recently met on a blind date. He had come to the door the night of their meeting and Keisha, as always, heralded the arrival of someone at the door with a string of barks and a charge down the stairs to the front door, skidding along the marble floor till the door interrupted her forward speed. She barked rabidly until the door opened, at which point she would greet and inspect the visitor. That night I was in my room on the third floor and heard the ceremonial barking: woo, woo, woo. The stampede-of-one down the stairs and the collision with the front door followed. Normally, after her greeting and inspection she came back upstairs with me and resumed her position by my side. But I noticed that she stayed downstairs until Julia and James had left. I heard the door close and finally she arrived back in my room, but I didn't think much of it at the time.

Their date that night had been nice, but both had agreed that no spark seemed evident. However, Julia felt he would be a wonderful addition to the friend list and she initiated that entry by including him in the birthday party.

A week later, Julia and I were busy on the phone at work planning the birthday celebration when she informed me of all the details that James was handling. I was impressed.

We had decided on deli sandwiches for the picnic and James was coordinating.

"He wants to know if you want black olives," Julia relayed on the phone that morning.

I had forgotten to include those on my order.

"So glad he thought of that," I said. I had a very particular list of ingredients for my preferred tuna sandwich. This man clearly understood details.

When James arrived that night for the birthday celebration, the doorbell rang and the Keisha-welcoming launched. Julia was still in her room so I followed the cacophony of dog-greetings to the lower level where Keisha danced in circles and jumped at the door.

"Good grief, Keisha. Let me open it!"

I managed to maneuver around the excited dog and upon opening the door I came face to face with a tall man with very blue eyes. I stopped to take in this person who seemed oh, so familiar to me. I tried to scan my brain for the name of this recognizable man but I was distracted by the whirls of *eeps* and *peeps* and jumping fur. He bent down immediately and Keisha jumped into his arms, almost knocking him over. She licked his face in a frenzy of dog-kisses and he received them with a grace and openness that was notable.

It seemed as if they already knew one another very well.

'Hi, there," I said, feeling a bit like I was interrupting something.

He put Keisha down and stood up, extending his hand to me.

"I'm James," he said, simply. "You must be Lily." He seemed caught off guard, though, and looked a bit puzzled. I would learn later that he, too, was having a sense of déjà vu and was trying to locate the source of the familiarity.

"You've met Keisha before?" It seemed like I was stating the obvious.

"Absolutely. Last week. When I picked Julia up for the animation festival," he smiled and looked down at her. She smiled and looked up at him.

Keisha escorted us up the stairs to the kitchen where Julia was organizing all the paraphernalia for the outing. We gathered the cake, the blankets and the cooler and carried them downstairs to James's car while Keisha kept jumping up on his legs trying to offer more kisses. She knew no restraint when it came to her affections. While she continued to assault her new love-interest with her unabashed ardor, I tried not to stare at him. But I needed to figure out where I had met him before.

James's black convertible was loaded with the items for the evening and he and Julia pulled away from the condo as Keisha and I watched. I would follow later with some friends.

I looked down at Keisha who seemed a bit forlorn that her new beau had driven away with another woman.

"Come on, girl. I'll feed you your kibbles and then I'll turn on some Vivaldi."

Keisha's love of Vivaldi was discovered a few months earlier not long after I had purchased a CD set of the great classical composers. Our well-appointed, ocean-view condo included a decadent steeping tub in the master bath and I often indulged in a long soak before bed. Recently I had added classical music as an accompanist to the event. Normally Keisha steered clear of anything related to baths, even if she were not the one involved, but I noticed once Vivaldi began to play she ventured into the bathroom, plopped down on the tile floor, and rolled onto her back. Her back legs splayed out while her front paws rested on her belly. Her eyes closed as she let the violin, violas and harpsichord wash over her, delighting in the seasonal interlude. No other composer was afforded the same audience.

So while Keisha settled in for an evening concert of Vivaldi, I headed down to the bay for an evening with Tchaikovsky.

The night was wonderful, the summer weather perfect. The bay was calm and reflected the sailboats that moored near the edge of the water to listen to the music. The sounds of the instruments filled the night air with the great composer's famous and not-so-well-known works.

The tuna sandwich was everything I had hoped.

James and I sat next to one another and began the evening with normal trivial conversation. I told him of my boyfriend living miles away while he explained that he was divorced, but didn't really have time for much dating. But as Tchaikovsky's music played through the night, our conversation continued and moved along a wide expanse of topics. We stopped briefly when we cut Julia's cake, picking right back up where we had left off. At the end of the night, we gathered our things and started the long walk back to our cars. Our conversation continued until we reached my car where we said goodnight.

As the marathon conversation ended, he took the initiative.

"I've really enjoyed talking with you. I feel like it's just started and there's more to go," he stated. "Would you like to meet sometime for lunch and continue it a bit?"

For some reason, his offer took me by surprise.

"Sure," I replied, feeling a bit like I was standing on one foot. "I know that you and Julia are friends. Should we invite her too?" I seemed to be stepping into some sort of girlfriend code.

"Absolutely. Why don't you check with her and I'll give you both a call early next week"

We said goodnight and I got in my car to head home to a waiting Keisha. She had been left out of the celebration, but I didn't think she really minded. She seemed content, nonetheless.

Chapter 24

> *"Piglet sidled up to Pooh from behind. 'Pooh!' he whispered. 'Yes, Piglet?' 'Nothing,' said Piglet, taking Pooh's paw. 'I just wanted to be sure of you.'"*
> — A.A. Milne,
> The House at Pooh Corner

He did call early the next week and the three of us met for dinner and a movie. Our offices were close to one another so the following week we met for lunch at a tiny restaurant in La Jolla overlooking the beach. Julia had given her blessings to James' and my budding friendship; she was dating someone new and was happy that James and I shared so many interests.

The easy flow of conversation continued at the lunch and we planned to meet for another outing soon. Within a month we were spending a lot of time together, talking about deeper things, including our past. We gathered at the dinner table weekly, sometimes more often. The coming together of two friends.

We explored new restaurants each week and ventured down our respective histories. The absence of a romantic aspect in the relationship seemed to take any pretenses away. While we both had felt a strong sense of familiarity when we met, we chalked it up to doppelgangers from our pasts. But I was not sure that was the only explanation as to the comfort level I felt with him.

We shared our life stories over wine and food and would often be politely asked to leave the restaurant as we had pushed way past the closing hour. He had been married at a very young age and after ten years of unhappiness, he and his ex-wife had decided to divorce. The emotional extrication from that relationship had been long and hard, he said.

"I have a hard time with goodbyes, I guess," he stated, flatly.

Oh, I knew that feeling, too.

It had been four years since they had officially divorced and he still carried scars from the relationship. He was surprisingly open and honest with some of his pain, but there was a natural flow in his revelations. And I received it without feeling uncomfortable.

I, too, shared my past including the seven years with *him* along with the entanglements that held me past the end of that relationship. I spoke of Dave but did not reveal too much, as I was not even sure myself as to what was going on. We shared many of our vulnerabilities and the immediate ease with which we had initially felt settled into something contented and safe. He had been a police officer briefly in his twenties, but was now in the corporate world. I noticed, though, the aura of the protective cop still hovered around him.

His relationship with Keisha held a similar comfort level and their friendship progressed along with ours, although technically Keisha met him first and had known him longer. The ex-cop did not realize yet, I thought, that his new friend had criminal tendencies or at the very least pushed the boundaries of existing rules. He joined us on our walks and she jumped into the back of his convertible as if she owned it. While rides in my little car were enjoyed with her head hanging out the passenger window, James's car afforded a full body experience. 180-degrees of both wind and smells.

Dave and I talked by phone often and I shared with him my budding friendship with James. Dave, too, had forged a similar friendship with a coworker, but his trips to California were fewer and I didn't have enough vacation days to travel to him. Or, at least, that was my excuse.

The months went by and James and I fell into a constant place in our lives. We spent much of our free time together, yet despite the depth of our connection we kept our relationship free of anything other than friendship. Keisha, on the other hand, had jumped full force into her love affair with James. She didn't really seem to have time for, or care about, my intentions with him.

My job required occasional travel, usually within California, and late in November I was scheduled to travel to the bay area for three days. With James's office less than a mile from my condo, I decided to ask him to check on Keisha at lunch, as I often did, during the days I would be gone.

"No problem," he said. "What time will she expect me?" Always a stickler for the details of life, he asked pertinent questions to make sure all expectations were met. Schedules were arranged, keys exchanged and Keisha was ready for a few lunch dates with one of her favorite people on earth.

That evening, as I sat in my seat on Amtrak's route to northern California, I closed my eyes and thought back to the last few months. It had been a layered and comforting roll-out of what was proving to be a deep and deeply satisfying friendship with James. He seamlessly had entered our lives and Keisha might have reminded me that she found him first!

The sound of the train tracks and the rocking of the car lulled me into further relaxation and I smiled. Life right now was good, regardless of wherever it was going. Things rarely turned out like I had planned but often took me in directions I had not expected and were frequently, surprisingly better. My reverie was interrupted by the faintest smell of incense. It seemed out of place in the vibrating train compartment. I sniffed the air intently and recognized it as my favorite scent often burned during my Tuesday night yoga class, which I was missing at that very moment. The class had become a staple of my week. No matter how tired or stressed I might feel, walking into the incense-filled room with the soft recording of tambura music never failed to shift me into a calmer internal place.

I looked at my watch: 7:42pm. My yoga class had started 12 minutes ago and everyone was probably moving out of Shavasana into the first pose. I clearly smelled the incense and I looked around the train-car to see from where it might be coming. I visually scanned the aisle: no tell-tale smoke wafted through the cabin. I stood up and scanned the rows of seats from one end to the next: just the heads of my fellow passengers, absorbed in their books or sleep. I shivered a bit in response to the air pushing down from the vent above me. Or maybe from the presence of the familiar smell.

When I arrived in San Jose after 1:00 am and checked into my hotel, I immediately called James to see how his noon visit with Keisha had gone. I knew that calling so late was perfectly okay; it spoke to our closeness.

"Things went great," he said sleepily. I could hear him smile. "We had a little outing."

"Oh?" I felt a little jealous. She and I always shared a hasty snack sitting on the couch at noon.

"We put the top down on the convertible and headed to Roberto's. I thought she might enjoy a snack too, so we grabbed some food and ate it down by the beach."

The man of details, I thought.

"She got food too?" I asked. It was a kind gesture to extend the well-check visit to include an impromptu picnic, but I was a bit annoyed that the fare was less-than-wholesome. I was usually strict with her diet.

"Two beef tacos. She loved 'em."

I'm sure she did—fast food, a ride in a convertible and a beachside picnic with a kind, caring and handsome man. Who wouldn't love that?

Chapter 25

"All I'm saying is that somewhere out there is the man you are supposed to marry. And if you don't get him first, somebody else will, and you'll have to spend the rest of your life knowing that someone else is married to your husband."

— Marie, on the difficulty of being single
When Harry Met Sally

Conversations with James meandered from trivial subjects to, more often than not, deeper explorations. It was refreshing to meet someone who seemed as overly-analytical as I was, although he seemed more pragmatic. Our musings often transpired over a meal. We had set aside Thursdays as our standing date to explore a new restaurant each week, and we took turns picking up the check. One night over Afghan food, the topic of relationships stepped forward as the entrées were being placed before us. We had already shared much about our past—the failures, the betrayals.

"One of my favorite movies is *When Harry Met Sally*," he offered. Movies were another shared passion and I thought the conversation was going to head in that direction. "The way those two characters met and got to know one another was refreshing. The physical attraction part was not involved. It was just two friends getting to know one another."

In the end, of course, those two friends became MORE than friends.

I agreed. It was a great story.

"That's the kind of relationship I want," he said, pointing his index finger, as if choosing a preferred flavor of ice cream. "One like that."

My spine straightened a bit by the energy coming off his statement.

I thought back to all the afternoons I had spent in the Cove Theater watching that movie. I agreed it was a good film and, yes, that kind of relationship would be great.

"It was a good film on so many levels," I said. "For some reason, I kept going back again and again to see it when I first moved here." I felt comfortable enough with him to admit how many times I sat alone in a theater watching the same movie over and over. "There was something about the humor, the scenes of New York, the back-and-forth between Harry and Sally."

He nodded in agreement.

"But I think at least part of the attraction was the theater itself," I said. "The Cove."

And . . . I also went time and time again because I was lonely, I thought to myself.

"That's where I saw it too!" he said. "One afternoon Carolyn Miller and I decided we had been working too many hours so we took the afternoon off and walked down the street to see it." The Cove Theater was only a block from James's office.

"Well, I might have been sitting a few rows in front of you. I certainly saw it enough times."

We laughed at the thought of possibly being in the same movie at the same time. I had always had an odd, almost savant-like ability with regard to dates and I rattled off the probable days I sat perched in the cool, dark theater with Harry and Sally—the only people I knew in San Diego at the time.

"I always saw it on a weekday. I always went to the 2 o'clock showing. It had only been out a week when I first started going to see it."

We did some mathematical computations and determined that yes, the probability of our being there at the same time was fairly high. There always seemed to be odd coincidences or synchronicities in our paths. I watched his hand, tanned and rough, grab the glass filled with icy water. I thought back to the night long ago as I sat across from *him*, in the bar, in Houston. His glass had held something a lot stronger than water.

"Do you believe in soulmates?" he asked, interrupting my flashback.

I was struck by the question and stopped for a moment. Was that a line from the movie? I couldn't remember.

"You mean is there one person that we are meant to be with?" I could feel the skepticism that had been growing in me the last few years sit up and join the conversation.

"Yeah. You think that there's some sort of destiny? That you're supposed to meet this one person?"

"And that there will be a happily-ever-after?" The cynic was now fully engaged.

"Well, I'm not a big believer in the fairytale aspect of that question. But I mean that *in general* the relationship is good and sound," he said.

So evidently he believed in the concept. I wondered where he thought HIS soulmate was at this very moment. Maybe she was sitting in the restaurant somewhere, just like I had been sitting in the theater—a future player in his life.

"I guess I believe in soulmates, plural." I realized I had never actually verbalized this fairly new feeling. "A few years ago I would have said, sure, 'Yes, there is THE someone out there for everyone.' But I don't know if I believe that now." The cynic was now ordering another glass of wine.

I stopped and he watched my face. I couldn't read his face in the dimly lit restaurant, but I was too busy hearing myself lay out this realization anyway.

"The notion that there is just one person in the entire world that is your destiny was certainly something I used to think." I stopped and my thoughts went back to the last few painful years. "But now I think it's not so black and white."

I watched the ex-cop's eyes take in my words. He was very still and his look was piercing. I thought it ironic that those eyes that had seen a lot of awful reality from behind his badge still allowed for such an idealistic thought. My own relatively sheltered life had not stopped me from hopping over to the cynical side of things when it came to love. He waited for me to continue.

"I have friends in my life that I believe are soulmates. It was destiny that we should meet. And I treasure having them. It almost seems mystical." I thought of Keisha. "And they don't even need to be human!"

I smiled and an ear-to-ear grin flashed across his face. He knew who I was speaking about.

"And when it comes to romantic love, I think that there ARE certain love relationships that are more soul-oriented than others." He knew who I was speaking about here, too.

"But no, I don't think there is just one." I was pretty sure I was right. "And you?"

I was pretty sure I knew his thoughts, but was interested to hear his words. I valued his opinion more than most. Maybe more than anybody.

"I do believe in one soulmate." He said it with the authority of a police officer sworn to uphold the laws of the land. He seemed resolute and sure of the statement. "Yes, I do."

Something about the way he said it made further conversation on the topic unwelcome.

"Well," he said rubbing his hands together and sitting up straight in the booth. "You ready to get the check and we can head out of here?"

No dessert tonight; it had been a big meal. I was working on digesting it all. As we walked out of the restaurant, I felt a tinge of jealousy—that James knew there was *the one* out there, waiting for him.

That Christmas Keisha gave James a special gift to thank him for his friendship. His condo north of San Diego overlooked the ocean and the corner balcony was sparsely decorated with one beach chair. What was a besotted dog supposed to gift her crush? Keisha and I had decided that the most perfect present for James would be a set of wind chimes for his balcony. Keisha loved going to James's and we headed there early one Saturday morning to present him with the package wrapped in bright red paper. She trotted up the stairs to his living room and vaulted onto his couch, resting on her favorite pillow. He opened the package and his face revealed that we had indeed selected the right thing. She watched as he removed the chimes from the box and we all walked outside for the ceremonial hanging. The morning was cool, crisp and sunny and the briny ocean smell clung to the morning breeze. The strings and the metal tubes twisted and turned and found their center. The wind picked up and danced with the chimes, transforming into the lightest melody.

We all three stood there, watching, listening to nature's concert.

"It reminds me of a song," he said, turning his head a bit like Keisha often did. "Give me a minute."

The wind had stopped but then surged forward again. His ears were tuned.

"Got it! It's the first strains of *The Girl from Ipanema*," he announced.

I listened. At first I couldn't hear it but he was right. It was clearly the first bar of the song,

We stood and listened as the wind played a repeat performance.

"How perfect! It's from Keisha, whose excitement comes out as *eeps* and *peeps*." We often laughed about that aspect of her.

"So my wind chimes play the song *The Girl from Eep-Eep-Ipanema!*" We both laughed and Keisha wagged her tail. It was then that Keisha's first nickname emerged. And somehow it seemed appropriate that her theme song was a bossa nova—some quick footwork, some good hip action.

And I had just learned of James's odd skill—he could, very quickly, convert the lyrics of any song into something applicable to whatever was at hand.

And he shared his latest version of Astrud Gilberto's song:

Short and black and young and fuzzy,
The girl from eep-eep-Ipanema goes walking
And when she passes,
Each squirrel she passes
She bites

I laughed and Keisha's tail wagged furiously. I thought she must have liked the part about squirrels. James's smile reached all the way to his blue eyes. It seemed we had chosen the perfect gift. And that moment of laughter could have fallen into the same category.

Chapter 26

"Nothing in all those 'O swan' poems had ever mentioned that they hissed...... Or resented being mistaken for felines........Or bit."
— Connie Willis,
To Say Nothing of the Dog

Dave visited that January. We had planned to go skiing in Mammoth, but we both came down with a nasty case of the flu and spent the week of his visit sick and miserable. The fever, the aches and pains, the stomach-upset, all crowded out any opportunity for real conversation. The time we had allotted for our trip was a disappointment on the surface, but was representative of a deeper illness that was now readily apparent in our situation and our relationship. *No time for skiing*, the universe seemed to say. *You need to address what is standing in the middle of the room.*

The following months we began to speak of it on the phone. I was relieved. He was relieved. But the relief did not make it any less painful. Neither of us wanted to say goodbye, even though staying was not working either. After we had talked through our reluctance and then final decision to part ways, Dave broached a surprising subject.

"I hate to say this, but one of the things I feel saddest about is not seeing Keisha anymore," he said sheepishly.

How sweet, I thought.

And then I realized I must have rested a notch below my dog in Dave's life.

"How funny," I answered, thinking the call was winding to a close and at a loss for an appropriate response. Keisha had been sleeping on the floor in a pool of sunlight and seemed oblivious that this heavy, sad conversation was now focused on her.

He sounded like he was reluctant to say something else. "Do you think that I can continue keeping in contact with Keisha?" His voice relayed how absurd his request sounded.

Good grief, I thought. Breakups were always hideous things to live through but this was too much. There's another woman and it's my DOG?

But I knew how much he loved her.

"Ummmm, I guess. What do you mean, exactly," I sighed.

"I'm going to be in San Diego, periodically, to visit Joe. And Tom and Angela have already asked me to be in their wedding. I was thinking that when I'm in town I could come pick her up, and we could go to the park, go for a run. Pick up some donuts. That kind of thing."

I looked at my sleeping dog. Was I going to need to buy a calendar for her social outings? I rolled my eyes. It seemed we were negotiating visitation rights.

"Sure. No problem." I wasn't really sure, but his request caught me off guard and my people-pleasing reflexes answered swiftly.

I heard him sigh and could feel the relief on the other end of the phone. The whole conversation was draining and we mercifully ended the call. THAT was the strangest break-up I had yet to encounter.

So a few days before my thirty-first birthday, I was officially single although it appeared Keisha still had deep connections near the Canadian border.

Maybe I would never find my partner, I thought. Maybe I should be happy with all the good that was already here.

But children. Oh, I wanted children. I had wanted to be a mother my entire life.

I sat on our patio, overlooking the ocean. The air was tangy with salt and the thick, pungent smell of the "red tide" that washes ashore seasonally. I couldn't see the red algae blooming from where I sat, it colored the water a dirty-red and lit up the tide with a luminescence at night, but I could detect it with my nose.

I must be a real Californian now.

I sat with my sadness, my fear of not attaining my goal of a child, and with the ocean. And with Keisha, splayed on the patio floor. James would be arriving soon to take me to dinner. The thought was comforting. He knew pain too and he would lend a compassionate ear to my dark thoughts.

I heard Keisha sigh.

Several months went by with little change in life other than a subtle awareness of the barrier that was now lifted between James and me with regard to our relationship. Everyone around us kept watching to see when we took those steps together into a different level of our deep friendship.

"Come on, already," our friends said.

Keisha, I believe, had the same sentiments.

But we were not going to be rushed. Things needed to move in their own time.

Dave did make an appearance on several occasions when he was in town. True to his word, he arranged for dates with Keisha. We both seemed at peace with the resolution of our relationship, and he and Keisha seemed more than pleased with continuing their dalliance. He would drop her off after their outing and relay the adventures they had. She did not stick around for de-briefing. She jogged upstairs, tired but happy for time spent with her good friend.

I felt no jealousy with their continued relationship. I had grown accustomed to the plethora of connections Keisha forged with others, separate from me. She was charming and skilled at flirtation. But my relationship with her may have been the only one in my life where I did not feel the threat of loss from the affections of another. Past betrayals and the fear of future ones held no power in my connection with her. It wasn't something I could pin-point. Someone else could surely ply her with tacos or French fries. Someone else may offer long walks or outings in the car. But I knew, deep in my core, that our relationship was betrayal-proof. It was an odd sensation that was new to my heart.

Later that summer, Keisha, James and I drove to Big Bear Village for a weekend of hiking and rest. Perhaps it was the change of scenery or the absence of all of those who had been watching and urging us on. Maybe it was the mountain air and the exercise. Maybe it was the rhubarb pie James had to make after he lost a bet over my odd ability to remember dates.

"What day of the week was June 7, 1972?" He threw out the challenge over our pancake breakfast on the patio of a restaurant down the street from our cabin.

Keisha's leash was clipped to a chair and she watched the exchange. Her black eyes looked at me.

I did the calculations in my head, extrapolating dates from my life that acted as markers for my internal calendar.

"It was a Wednesday."

Keisha looked at James as if to say, *Really? You haven't learned yet?*

A post-breakfast walk to the local library confirmed my weird talent. And James was off to the grocery store to buy the ingredients for my favorite pie. That weekend we decided, in an unspoken way, that we were ready. We returned from the San Bernardino Mountains that Sunday night ready to explore a new phase. The cautious parts of us had circled each other long enough. We stepped into the romantic arena and as with most things in our relationship, it was easy and comfortable.

Keisha and I soon moved our things north to James's condo, where the wind chimes continued to play Keisha's theme. We transitioned to our new household easily and settled into a comfortable, lighthearted routine —just the three of us. Time moved quickly and within a year our situation transitioned to the next phase.

We were engaged.

Shortly before the surprise event, I awoke from my long-dormant wedding dream. The nightmare had been blissfully silent since Dave and I had parted ways, but this night it returned. Only this time, it was different. I was not getting ready for the wedding. I was not in the car going to the church. I wasn't at the altar looking at my faceless groom. No Mission Impossible theme played in the background. The ceremony had happened! The rings were on the selected fingers. The reception had played out in a festive, celebratory way.

The dream progressed to the quiet after the momentous event. I was tired but happy from a long day of festivities and I stood in front of a closet, holding my wedding dress on a hangar. I opened the dark closet door and light shined across the dowel that stretched from one side to the other. It was empty except for this treasured article that I placed ceremoniously in its new home. I looked at the dress—the shoulders pushed out from the metal hangar—and realized the mission was complete! I was married and I felt good.

But while my dreams were sorting through the compartments of my psyche, Keisha had been a participant in planning events during the waking hours.

James had kept her updated on the purchase of the ring and the surprise proposal planned for a trip to Carmel and San Francisco over the Thanksgiving holiday. James dropped to his knees on a cold and rainy day-after-Thanksgiving in Ghirardelli Square. The Center's Christmas tree had been lit, and a live band was playing Christmas carols. My fear of marriage had vanished, and there was not an ounce of hesitation in saying *yes*. As soon as the ring was placed on my finger, the first person notified was Keisha. She had stayed behind with Julia in our old condo, where she often vacationed when James and I traveled. My mother was the second call placed, behind Keisha, but I didn't feel the need to let my mom know that Keisha's notification had priority over the bride's mother.

That night over a celebratory dinner, sipping champagne that was obscenely expensive, James raised a toast to our new adventure and said, "You know, Keisha was involved in all of this." He seemed pleased he had an accomplice. "She knew where I had hidden the ring." He smiled.

I smiled back, knowing that his statement was true.

"When you were at yoga class the other night, I was packing for the trip and hiding the ring in my suitcase. I took the ring box, opened it and showed it to Keisha who had been sitting on the bed overseeing things."

"Did she approve?"

"She sniffed it. Then licked it delicately. So that would be an affirmative." The policeman smiled.

I looked down at the ring, now on its permanent new home—my left hand. The diamond sparkled in the candlelight of the restaurant. I smiled too, knowing that it had Keisha's stamp of approval.

Wedding plans began almost immediately.

My mother had practically swooned when she heard the news that there was to be a wedding. I think she was convinced that I would never marry. Even though I was in my mid-thirties my mom was going to assist with the planning.

One Saturday morning, she and I gathered on the phone with calendars, magazines and pen and paper for a long-distance wedding-planning session. Dates, venues, food, and dresses were all dissected and discussed. I hesitantly broached a subject I had not felt strong enough to bring up before. I tightened my jaw and jumped in.

"I was thinking about having Keisha as one of my bridesmaids."

The cat (or dog, in this case) was now out of the bag.

The silence on the phone was blaring and long. In fact, I thought we might have been disconnected.

"Hello? Mom? Are you still there?"

"I'm here," she said, her answer stern. THIS was why I had not wanted to bring up the subject. I silently blessed the 1,400 miles that separated the two callers.

More silence.

"You can't be serious," she said. "She's a dog."

"She's my best friend." I could almost sense my mother putting down her pen, adjusting herself in her seat and squaring her shoulders. She clearly loved me, but at times her daughter needed some straightening out.

"What's she going to do? Walk down the aisle? Stand at the altar? Pose for pictures?" Her voice was rich with sarcasm. I think it was the only tool she had available to deal with the nonsense I had presented.

"Well, yes, actually." The fewer words the better, I thought.

My mother sighed. I knew how much she loved Keisha, that love had been forged through good times and teeth-gnashing clashing of wills. But I was stepping into sacred territory that belonged to the mother-of-the-bride. I felt badly that my mom couldn't physically participate in the planning. I knew she would have loved it more than I—going to the florist, taste-testing cakes, dress shopping. And now I was depriving her of something that seemed to be a given in her book—a dog-free wedding.

"Never mind," I said. "It was just a thought. She'd probably steal the show anyway. Or poop at the altar."

I was the only one who felt strongly about wanting Keisha to be included. I'm sure it didn't matter to her. The rules, regulations and general restrictions of a formal affair were not on her list of fun so I let it go.

"Thank Goodness," my mother sighed. Her relief flowed through the phone line. Keisha was on a walk with James at that moment and would never know she had just been relieved of her bridesmaid duties.

We decided we wanted an outdoor venue, beside the ocean, and we began scouting sites downtown and on Coronado Island. My preference would have been the Hotel Del Coronado, the historic resort where I purchased my magic wand many years before. But finances continued to be a constraint, so we chose a resort across the island with a bay view that looked over the park where we had Julia's birthday. The site had an open grassy area that stretched down to the water's edge and a beautiful pond close to the hotel building where regal swans glided across the water and roamed the grounds. Their long, graceful necks and white feathers added a fairy-tale quality to the setting.

One Saturday morning James and I decided to head down to Coronado to take some measurements of the space for the rental of a tent and dance floor. It was a sunny, crisp day and we decided that Keisha would enjoy the outing. The top came down on the convertible and we trundled down the freeway and across the bridge to Coronado.

Once there, Keisha hopped from the car and pranced with great authority to the grounds where the sidewalk curved towards the swan pond. A bevy of swans glided gently along the surface of the water, which sat between the hotel building and the concrete slab where our reception would be held under a large white tent. A public park sat adjacent to the reception site, and today was filled with children climbing on the wooden play structure, families picnicking, and people throwing balls and Frisbees along the wide expanse of grass. I was glad we had brought Keisha. She would enjoy it, too.

As we approached the pond a couple of swans arched their necks to watch Keisha trot forward on the path. Her speed picked up and clearly a connection had been made. At that moment Keisha kicked into a full gallop heading straight to the pond, barking a none-too-friendly greeting at the swans. Despite their elegant and genteel look, swans were known to be notoriously unfriendly. And this aspect of their nature rose with a fury to meet Keisha's initial salvo. I was being pulled helplessly along with Keisha's charge and the swans began screeching and flapping their wings. Chaos ensued in the once serene pond, water flying in all directions. Swans scattered from the pond and charged forward to the sidewalk where Keisha was straining at her leash to meet them. She emitted deep, foreboding growls between loud, piercing barks.

Having been present at more than one altercation initiated by Keisha, I knew things could escalate quickly.

This did not bode well.

James raced forward and intercepted Keisha's charge against the swan brigade. He scooped her up in his arms, stopping her forward progress. The swans continued to scream and Keisha met their cries with ferocious barking. James yelled at the swans to stop and stood his ground. His previous police training had taught him to take command of the dangerous and chaotic situation, and the swans seemed to respond to his directive.

Keisha continued to snarl and bark; she wasn't giving up. Heads were turning in the park as the ruckus cast a spotlight on the noisy animal exchange.

We had created quite the brouhaha upon our arrival.

The swans reluctantly retreated to the water, and we headed back to the park. Keisha continued her dialogue with the swans over James's shoulder until she was ceremoniously plopped into the backseat of the car. Disorderly conduct in a public place might have been the charge.

I was now even more comfortable with the decision to leave Keisha at home during the wedding.

The wedding started at 1:00p.m. on a sunny, warm October Sunday. My father and I stood at the back of the historical building, a one-hundred-year-old Jewish temple now maintained by the Parks and Recreation Department. My right arm wound around my dad's and I looked to the front of the building at the retired Episcopal minister standing in front of the opening in the wall where the Torah was placed all those years ago. He smiled, waiting to perform the ceremony we had crafted with his help. The bride, who didn't believe in fairy tales, was dressed in a white lace and tulle gown reminiscent of a princess's dress. I held a small, tightly-bound bunch of yellow roses, a nod to my Texas roots.

It was an eclectic mix.

I smiled at my dad as the harpist played the last few notes of "All I Ask of You" from Phantom of the Opera and my eyes traveled again to the front of the room where the wedding party stood. Unlike my recurring nightmare, I was not running escape routes through a frantic mind. There was no face-less, unwanted groom waiting at the end of the aisle.

Instead, I was getting ready to take the first step forward with confidence and excitement, to walk through the loved ones gathered in the pews, and join the smiling, blue eyes of James. To grab his arm and exchange vows that my nightmares warned me I should avoid at all costs.

Yet as my focus shifted to my waiting groom, I scanned the rows of people gathered in the tiny, creaky building with arched, leaded glass windows. There was my mom and my grandmother. My aunts and uncles. All had traveled from Texas. My cousins. Sydney, Julia, Anna, and Ali. Other friends and coworkers. There were James's parents, his sister all smiling, waiting for me to join their family. More friends. More loved ones. Each held a special place in our lives.

I could feel the excitement from the front of the room: James, the minister and the wedding party. But it took me a moment to recognize what I felt from those sitting in the old wooden pews. They smiled and waited. I turned my head slightly to discern the feeling. It was a tangible feeling, one of love, that I felt coming from the participants. They had all been part of our journey so far, joining James and me at different parts of our lives. And they had traveled here today to share in this long-awaited, beautiful moment. James and I may have been the stars of the show but this was an ensemble production. Their participation, unspoken support and love filled the room and changed the air that wafted through the open windows.

It caught my breath.

At that moment, the harpist struck the first cords of The Wedding March and my father and I took our first step into the gathering.

The ceremony was brief and I felt cocooned by the setting and the warmth that filled the small space. Finally the minister turned to the gathering and said directly to them: "One of James's and Lily's favorite movies is *When Harry Met Sally*. In it, the character Harry Burns said, 'When you realize you want to spend the rest of your life with somebody, you want the rest of your life to start as soon as possible.' So without further ado, I present to you Lily and James Erickson."

After the ceremony our group gathered under the large outdoor tent beside the water to enjoy cocktails, an early dinner and a San Diego sunset. The bay was glistening with the churning of passing boats and lumbering Navy ships returning to port. The air smelled of salt water and of the delectable foods emerging on china plates, carried by waiters in starched white shirts and black pants. The tinkling of glass joined the sounds of the water lapping against the shore.

The cake was cut, the champagne poured and the music began to flow.

I joined James on the dance floor for our first dance. I worried I might feel awkward being the only couple moving and twirling along the floor. But like my awareness in the church, I felt at home and at ease with everyone gathered there, watching the bride and groom and sharing our moment.

As the music played I leaned into James's shoulder. "What a day! It's beautiful. Everything is perfect," I said, whispering into his ear. His hand squeezed mine in response.

"But I wish Keisha were here," I added, my brow furrowed. She was spending the day and the next two weeks of our honeymoon at Julia's. I could feel him pull back to look into my eyes. His face was quizzical, concerned.

"Really?" he questioned.

"Don't you?" I responded. The marriage was only a few hours old and I was already feeling irritated with my handsome groom.

While he kept guiding me across the floor in time with the music, he scanned the tables, laden with plates of savory chicken and vegetables, the bread baskets filled with plump, yeasty rolls waiting to be slathered with butter. His eyes moved to the cake table. Vanilla crumbs and lemon filling spilled from the center where eighty-something slices had been cut.

He looked back at me with raised eyebrows.

Non-verbal communication was beginning to be second nature to us.

I rolled my eyes in response.

"Yes, all very enticing, I know." I sighed. "She would be at every table asking to share in the delights."

"Chicken is her favorite, you know." He smiled and winked.

His eyes then directed mine to the pond, set twenty feet away from the gathered crowd. The swans glided through the water, their feathers calm and their heads held nobly atop their long necks. It was a scene of beauty and peace. He looked back at me once again with a questioning look.

"Yes, I get that too," I conceded. "I'm sure she would create a kerfuffle there, too."

I pictured the elegant birds screeching and spraying water as they answered the loud and pushy dog. The drama might have well moved under the tent to the starched table cloths, statuesque floral arrangements and well-dressed members of the party. Angry, wet birds and surly, combative dogs were not something that enhanced a wedding celebration.

He smiled and squeezed my hand again. He understood Keisha's and my connection. He clearly had compassion for my longing to share this gorgeous moment with my dear friend. But his years in law enforcement informed his practicality: you don't tempt fate and invite a bull into a china shop.

Keisha spent our wedding day snoozing on Julia's couch and caught up on the details of the affair that evening while munching leftovers from the party.

Chapter 27

"Everyone has a hidden talent. Some are just so well hidden that you can never find them."
— Susan Gale

The wedding had been a success and life continued on in its same comfortable way. It often felt to me that the three of us had joined forces legally and spiritually and that Keisha's name should have been on the marriage license as well. She held a deep abiding love for James and I often wondered if she considered me her *beard*, or stand-in, so that she could marry him.

I had begun to study Hatha Yoga, a system of physical postures and breath control, not long after I moved to San Diego. I started with a small class held in my teacher's living room. She was an ex-dancer and moved into teaching yoga many years ago, studying in ashrams in India. Being an ex-dancer myself, her past and approach resonated well with me. She guided us through the postures with special attention to alignment, to how the pose looked, striving to achieve the perfect position.

I remembered my mom buying a tiny book at the grocery store in the early '70s that had about fifteen yoga poses, or asanas, listed in the booklet. She would do the poses in our living room and I quietly watched, intrigued. A resurgence of yoga was happening in the early '90s, and I stumbled upon this class. My ego would not let me re-enter the dance world. It had been too long and my body would not let me compete in the way that my mind demanded. Yoga seemed like a great compromise.

As a dancer, I spent hours in front of the floor-length mirror. It was the feedback mechanism to ensure proper alignment, to achieve the much-strived-for-perfection. In the performance, the audience determined the success or failure of the dance. My internal feedback, which might be one of pain or injury, was always secondary.

Always.

It didn't matter what it felt like inside. The body must move perfectly in the choreographed path. The audience must be impressed. Pain was to be ignored.

Smile.

And be the outward perfection.

But in yoga, there was no mirror, no audience. My attention was brought inward and my body gave the direction—too far into a pose and the pain signaled potential injury, not far enough and the pose was not doing its work. It was walking a razor's edge to find the path, and it was all inner work. And it was new terrain to me.

Little-by-little, I opened to the depth of the practice. During the last decade of working in an office environment I had disconnected from my body in a way in which I was not even aware. It felt good to step out of the office uniform of heels, hose and suits and step into a baggy T-shirt and stretchy pants. As a dancer, I had never consciously coordinated my breath with specific movements of my body, but now this ancient practice was informing me of the marriage between movement and breath. I often watched it happen spontaneously with Keisha. Her movements were more cat-like than canine, but like all cats and dogs, she spent a lot of time stretching and yawning. It looked dance-like but un-choreographed, coming from a natural response and flow.

Shortly after we were married, I began taking classes at a yoga studio next to James's office. The classes were larger and the studio offered a teacher certification that was not available yet in many places. James had purchased my first module in the yoga teacher-training program as a gift. Yoga had been my savior on so many levels, moving and stretching my body in ways that unkinked its blocked and tight pathways. The incense and the chanting background music called to my Catholic upbringing, spending countless hours amidst the ceremony and ritual of that faith. I decided I would like to deepen my yoga practice by becoming certified to teach.

The twice-weekly classes were an intense journey into anatomy, the physical poses and study of the ancient yogic texts that attempted to explain the nature of our universe. We were required not only to have a daily Hatha yoga practice with various assigned postures, but we were also to meditate daily while keeping a journal of our experiences. While my body and mind celebrated in the daily yoga poses, they also rebelled against the meditation practice. My body did not like sitting still for even short periods of time. And my mind, directed to be calm, was given a mantra to quiet itself, but it raced at the speed of a comet.

My daily fifteen minutes of meditation felt agonizingly long and, at times, unbearable. I would park myself on the floor of our spare bedroom, atop a woolen blanket, and charge myself with entering into a state of deep connection with the universe and the Divine. No baby steps for me! The directive quickly turned to physical discomfort and an appallingly rebellious mind. Thoughts came fast and furious and flitted from one thing to another.

I focused on my breathing and things would calm down.

But soon the discomfort returned. My butt hurt and my left shoulder ached. I was thinking about the report that was due at work. How was I going to pay for the new car I needed? It seemed I was in constant battle with my desire for transcendence and my busy, chattering monkey-mind.

My teacher, Rama, with an otherworldly sense of peace about her, gently urged us on in our attempts at achieving what the ancient yogis wrote about so many centuries ago. We shared our struggles and our insights with each other, and I felt like I had stepped into something very important on my journey. We studied the Upanishads, the Yoga Sutras and The Vedas. The words resonated in me at my core. I had taken numerous philosophy and religious studies courses in college as electives. I was drawn to them like food. And now I felt like I had found the cuisine that I liked the best. It felt like home, even though I struggled so perplexingly with the simplest task of sitting still and watching my breath.

My daily meditation practice progressed and Keisha always took her place in front of me. My legs crossed in the lotus position, she lay facing me, her legs outstretched like a sphinx. With her head resting on her extended front legs, she watched me as I sat, eyes closed, and entered my fifteen-minute battle with my own interior thoughts, waiting for a transcendent experience.

This yogi, it seemed, was being observed.

Closing my eyes, I breathed in, watching the breath in my mind's eye as it traveled into my body and filled my lungs. I felt the tightness, the edges where the air that had been floating in the space around me sought to enter this restricted body. It was uncomfortable and my mind stepped in almost immediately. The chatter of my thoughts drowned out any sensations I was feeling in my body.

Judgment soon followed.

I breathed again, feeling the sensation of breath and the stillness. But thoughts barged in quickly and loudly and diverted my progress onto the path of transcendence.

I was a failure as a yogi.

So I followed the directions of my teacher and continued to bring my awareness back to my breath. And noticed the tightness again. Then the thoughts stepped in again. I continued this dance each night, as my competing partners of breath and thoughts grabbed for the next few steps. I flowed with each until the other demanded their turn.

It was an Argentine tango of push and pull.

And then one night the dance evolved from a dramatic Latin tango into a fluid waltz—my breath and the movements becoming a graceful and eloquent flow. My awareness of my body, that tight, restrictive mass of flesh seemed to dissolve and I was aware of the space around me. I could literally feel the room. It was solid, and yet vast and expansive. My awareness continued to move outward, beyond the walls of the condo, to the tree outside the window, then beyond the tree to the parking lot. It kept expanding, opening to the grassy slope leading to the street and beyond that. I was moving, feeling the space around me like Star Trek's *Enterprise* slicing through deep space.

At that moment, a loud bark pierced the air. My awareness came crashing back to my body. My heart pounded. My breath stopped from the surprise of the sound. My eyes flew open and Keisha stood in front of me, her dark eyes staring at me with an intensity I had not seen before, her tail wagging though.

My goodness, I thought.

I blinked and reoriented myself to the room—the bed, the dresser, the chair by the window. And the excited furry creature staring at me. My breath settled back into my body and my awareness nestled back into the space behind my eyes. Keisha moved toward me and sniffed the air around me. She seemed to be gathering information. After a while she stopped, returned to her spot on the carpet and resumed her position again.

I'm not sure what she had decided but the moment was over.

A few days later at my next class, I waited for a break to pull Rama aside and ask her thoughts on what might have happened that night.

She paused and thought for a moment. Rama had been a student of yoga for more than thirty years and had lived in an ashram in India for twenty of those. She seemed to be the embodiment of the peace that comes from a devoted immersion into a spiritual path. She never seemed judgmental or a know-it-all. She instructed with a calmness and presence that spoke to the truths that we were studying. She had invited us to test the yogic path and see what changes, if any, it might bring to our lives.

Normally I was one to view most people with a grain of distrust or at least discernment, but I had come to respect her few but thought-provoking words.

"There is a belief," she began, "that some lamas in the Tibetan path who don't quite achieve their earthly goals of enlightenment or complete detachment from their earthly existence are sent back in their next life as dogs. This path may teach them some of the finer points of their own journey."

I waited for her to continue, not quite sure where this was going.

"It may be that your dog is perceiving the changes in your energy system as you move deeper into your meditation." She stopped and quietly watched me as I digested this information.

"Okay," I said rather inadequately. I didn't have a folder with which to file this unexpected information, not even sure what I may have expected. I was aware of the body's energy system that eastern traditions teach as the chakras and I had seen renderings or even Kirlian photography of what some call our aura. But I had not necessarily equated any of this information within my own body, per se, and certainly had not put it in the same sentence with what my dog was perceiving.

I pictured what Keisha might be doing right now and for a moment, saw her in a different context than when I had left the house this morning.

Rama smiled and didn't seem inclined to have anything more to say. But she noted my continued silence, and what must have been a puzzled look on my face, and proceeded a bit more.

"It may be that as your body and your mind begin to calm down and you become more aware of the truer, more subtle nature of our existence, that the colors within your energy field, your aura, begin to change. Your frequency shifts and what you emanate from your electrical body may change. Keisha may be perceiving this change, and it may startle her."

That seemed to be all that she was offering me, but she sat calmly with me while I tried to absorb the information.

"Thank you," I offered. I really didn't know what else to say. She had presented something to consider about this little being that I thought I knew so well. She was suggesting a concept that was completely foreign to me.

I drove home still contemplating this bit of information. I thought back to the night, after my painting class, where I looked at the world with new eyes—a world of just lines, shapes and colors. Perceptions had shifted.

And now I was driving along the same highway with another shift in perception.

I didn't know much about Tibetan lamas. I knew of the most famous one, the Dalai Lama. His crinkling smile seemed to urge all of us to *lighten up*! He didn't just laugh, he chortled and it lifted my spirits just watching the joy that seemed to travel through his body. The Dalai Lama evidently had a humble beginning of his earthly body, born to farmers, but his royal spiritual lineage had placed him at the top of his Buddhist community. Keisha, as well, was a product of the royal-Chinese-guard-dog-lineage tainted by a few seconds of carnal pleasure by the scamp next door. No auspicious DNA flowed down her double-helix. But she, too, seemed to possess a good amount of the twinkling lightness that His Holiness demonstrated so well.

My image of monks and their cloistered lives didn't match up, in my mind's eye, with the gregarious, smiling Dalai Lama. I envisioned their lives devoted to chanting, deep meditation, silent chores in austere surroundings and a daily existence of simplicity, sacrifice and discipline.

I thought of Keisha and the implication that there may be more going on there.

IF she had been a lama, what kind of monk must she have been? It was an absurd thought, but I conjured a view that might place Keisha-the-lama in that quiet, contemplative and spiritually focused life. I envisioned the Keisha-monk, clad in ochre robes, moving silently through the halls of the monastery. Did her willful and sensory-driven personality express there as well? Did she sneak into the larders at night to steal extra food? Or even escape the boundaries of the monastery in search of donuts? Did her rule-breaking penchants find her skipping out of the long chants or dodging other duties? It was not a stretch to see how all those traits may have bound the wayward lama back to the earth for more training and another try at the art of self-discipline. If that were the case, things weren't going in the right direction in this incarnation either.

Good heavens, I thought, as I shook my head and turned off at the freeway exit to our condo. My imaginings seemed ridiculous and I laughed out loud. Yep, I concluded, if that poor lama had even a small portion of the undisciplined, pleasure-seeking, manipulative tendencies of my Keisha, then another life was indeed warranted to move along the path of enlightenment.

I pulled into the parking space beneath our second-floor living room window. Keisha sat perched on the back of the couch waiting for my return. She looked down at me, backlit by the living room lamp, and I looked up at the dark silhouette. I wondered what she perceived now. I stared at the dark figure, looking at me. The cool night air made me shiver. After a moment, she sailed off the couch and disappeared from my view as she ran to meet me at the front door.

Tail wagging, her sparkling eyes still greeted me in her usual way but I had the slightest sense now that there might be just a little more behind those dark eyes.

Chapter 28

*"Do your practice
and all is coming."*
— Sri K Patthabi Jois

My yoga training continued in earnest and I felt like my body and my spirit were being massaged from the inside out. I continued my daily asanas along with my meditation. My homework was to teach the poses to others, too, and learn to adjust the asanas to meet their flexibility.

I ended my own practice each day with Shavasana, morbidly called the corpse pose, and almost always had James lay in the restorative position after our work. Keisha had begun to participate in Shavasana each time she saw one of us do it. She would calmly get up, seek out her lamb's wool bone, and every so gently place the toy on our chest, almost directly over the heart area. She then would walk cautiously to our head and curl up, snoot to tail, emitting a deep sigh. She would rest there for as long we stayed in the pose.

This impulsive dog, usually bounding with energy and a seemingly ever-present seeker of the next sensory adventure, shifted into a different persona at these times. Her expression moved to a pensive one and her brows almost seemed to furrow. She crossed the room and retrieved the fuzzy bone like a priest carrying the chalice towards the altar. Her movements were slow and graceful; her entire demeanor downshifted.

I had shared Rama's explanation with James as to Keisha's odd behavior during my meditation and we both laughed at the idea of Keisha's otherworldly abilities. We noticed her lambs-wool-toy-ritual with what we now referred to as "The Shavasana Bone" and often giggled when it happened. She seemed unfazed by our good-natured ribbing. Our house was fraught with the love of nicknames and there were many. We often referred to her as "The Garbage Girl", as she had a keen love of rummaging through garbage cans, and now her newest nickname emerged, based on her potential previous-life as a not-entirely-successful Tibetan lama: The Doggie Lama.

It seemed to fit her perfectly. She was indeed an imperfect being with her penchant for garbage diving, stealing snacks and utilizing her charms to get exactly what she wanted. And yet there were hints at her ability to operate at a deeper level in her connection to the world in an almost sublime way. Like most dogs, she had an equanimity of presence, of being fully in the moment, whatever it had to offer. But even beyond that I could sense in some unexplainable way that she knew my soul like no other being, human or animal. Perhaps she knew me better than I knew myself.

She knew it.
She touched it.
She nestled into it, snoot to tail.

My yoga training courses were offered in modules—some meditation-based, while others focused on the physical postures and the anatomy behind them. Those not enrolled in the certification process were allowed to participate in the individual courses and James joined me in the next meditation class.

We gathered weekly to read and study the ancient yogic texts and to explore the practice of meditation. Our teacher instructed us on various techniques to still the mind, to calm the body and, hopefully, to begin to have an experience that the Eastern traditions taught were of our true nature. Our homework was to meditate each day for fifteen minutes and to keep a journal. She had given simple directives to sit in the most comfortable position possible so that the mind was not focusing on discomfort. I had always been extremely flexible, so sitting in the traditional lotus posture—legs bent, crisscrossed and feet resting on my thighs—was an easy task. My husband was not so lucky.

James's musculature was strong and tight, and his limbs did not bend with any ease. Rama had shown him how to use pillows and bolsters to support his knees as well as his back.

"You don't want to spend the time you set aside focusing on how your body hurts!" she said.

So each night the three of us gathered for our allotted time to commune with the universe. Keisha and I took up roost in the dining room on the floor under the window. James opted to take his pillows and blankets, needed to quiet his orthopedic issues, and set up camp on the other side of the wall in the hallway. We settled in and I looked at the clock on the bureau.

"Okay," I announced. "Let's start."

And we invited in a greater awareness for the next fifteen minutes.

Keisha and I had been doing this ritual for a while and we quickly settled in. My body was quiet, while I started my nightly tango of breath and thoughts.

Things didn't seem too routine on the other side of the wall, however.

The sounds of pillows being fluffed, blankets being shifted. Arms and legs moving to find a better position.

Then quiet.

The absence of sound was vibrant and my thoughts began to calm again.

Then more sounds from behind the wall. More fluffing. More adjusting. A cough.

Then a settling followed by that delicious silence.

But the silence lasted mere moments. The sounds of discomfort resumed and I opened my eyes just enough to see if James had come into the room. It was empty except for Keisha, still in her reclining position. She too had opened one eye in response to the fitful noises behind the wall. She sighed. The rustling grew less and the periods of quiet became longer until the sound changed to something quite different. An audible snore wafted through the air, around the corner and into the space that Keisha and I shared.

Clearly James's body and his thoughts had found a comfortable space.

I smiled and peeked again at Keisha to share a knowing look. But the Doggie Lama, eyes closed, was deep in communion with the cosmos.

Chapter 29

*"Count your rainbows,
not your thunderstorms"*
— Unknown

Life tends to continue in a relentless way, sometimes for long stretches of contentment or even boredom, but then can change rather dramatically with various events. Then the journey becomes a bit more erratic as change is navigated.

A large corporation on the East Coast had negotiated the purchase of James's employer and gave him the choice of relocating to North Carolina or facing unemployment. While we realized we lived in an area many people referred to as paradise, we had become weary of the traffic, congestion and high prices. We began to talk of having a family and moving to a less dense area where the cost of living was significantly lower. We seriously considered the move.

On the long walks and drives by the beach, we often contemplated what it would be like to leave the area. It had been seven years since I had made the initial journey to what now felt like home, but those seven years seemed longer. My roots had grown deep here. And yet there was an enticement of something new, an opportunity to step beyond the current boundaries.

He accepted the position and was to begin work immediately. Keisha and I would stay behind for a couple of months to finish my work and my yoga training and to pack up our belongings.

So as James boarded the plane for North Carolina, Keisha and I found ourselves, just as we had been all those years ago in our little apartment on Lake Street, living together just the two of us. As much as we missed James, it was fun to spend those last San Diego days beside one of the most beautiful bodies of water, walking with my soul companion. We had a few short weeks to put the finishing touches, mentally and emotionally, on everything we had experienced up to this point. And then we were to embark on a new adventure.

The moving van pulled away from our condo overlooking the ocean around midnight. It had been a long day of boxes and moving men, clearing our home of all of its contents. When I had moved from Houston, I had few belongings and what I did have easily was transported to a storage room. But now we had accumulated rooms full of belongings and all our possessions were carefully stacked inside an enormous white truck. A massive painted blue arrow surged along the side of the van. *Things were moving*, the arrow proclaimed. As the truck holding our accumulation-of-things trundled across the

U.S., James, Keisha and I loaded our bags into the car and headed east.

My dog was a seasoned traveler by now and was used to seeing her earthly necessities packed into a plastic grocery bag—kibble and water bowls, Shavasana bone, rubber pork chop and her leash. This was all she needed on earth to feel safe and comfortable (and probably not even that). It was in stark contrast to the tonnage we had loaded onto the moving van.

Our journey east along Interstate 40 meandered among some dramatic scenery, the Western United States grand and imposing. As the Southwest flattened into the open plains in the center of the nation, the vistas stood long and somewhat monotonous. It was still a primal comfort to see vast areas of agriculture stretched out for miles on end. The plains gradually transitioned to the more dense foliage of the southeast, and the end of the summer offered hot and intense expressions of the season.

Keisha had become used to the idyllic, at times boring, consistency of Southern California's weather. On the rare occasions of rain, the gentle pitter-patter of the drops as they hit the roof were the only signal of the change in weather. Lightning and thunder were rarer and were distant and faintly heard. Our drive east was fraught with intense heat punctuated with breathtaking bouts of violent weather. The thunder and lightning seemed to be on top of the car as we were engulfed in blinding rain. Nature's fury catapulted her from the backseat into my lap where she would shiver and pant in an alarming way. I would hold her and soothe her, despite my own level of fear, but it did little to calm her.

She held not an ounce of courage in the face of dramatic weather.

We pulled into our new driveway four days later, and Keisha hopped out triumphantly, ready for the next phase of life. Her paws landed on the soft bed of pine needles that spread across the yard where the seventy-foot pine trees created a womb-like feeling and sheltered us from the intense sun. The heat and humidity were oppressive, but our excitement of setting up our new home was palpable. She trotted up the front steps, to the wooden porch so common in the south, and stood by the front door. She seemed to know this was home.

I had always been intrigued at the different styles of homes across our country. My Texas roots felt at home in the brick or stone ranch houses that sprawl lengthwise across wide lawns. Southern California was resplendent with Mediterranean or Spanish style homes with brightly painted stucco and tile roofs. The southeast offered a more colonial or early American flavor with wood siding and painted porches. The location's history often informed the architecture.

Walking through the door of our tiny cottage nestled among the pine trees just west of Chapel Hill, North Carolina, I could almost feel the tone of our lives change. James had settled into his work and Keisha and I set about unpacking and creating a new living space for our family. We ventured out for long walks, absent our beloved ocean. The piney woods were reminiscent of our walks in Houston along with the heat and humidity.

Keisha's first experience with squirrels occurred during her stay at my parent's home. The critters lived in the large oak trees surrounding the house and loved to frolic on the patio. She first spied them through the sliding glass door and had instantly determined they were not to be trusted and needed to be chased. They would taunt her through the glass, knowing she could not get them unless she was mercifully released through the door.

Then the fireworks flew.

But the squirrels had been left behind in Texas. In the beach areas where we lived in San Diego, there were very few and none in our condo complex. Keisha enjoyed a nice respite from the pests during those years. However, our move to the South reintroduced the varmints into our lives and Keisha was beyond agitated. As the squirrels twitched their tails to and fro, staring at my normally happy-go-lucky pet, Keisha would tremble with disdain, emit a guttural sound from her chest and bare her teeth. They were mortal enemies and this was war.

Summoning the rage that was building in her body, she would charge after them. They, in turn, sprinted across the lawn and skittered up the trees to a safe distance.

The battle was on. And Keisha's foe seemed to enjoy the clashes.

She stood at the base of the tree and intermittently barked and growled. The squirrels twitched their tails and peered down. Keisha's body quivered with rage.

There was a detectable smile on their squirrel-lips.

It took a couple of weeks to unpack the multitude of cartons that the big blue truck had delivered. As I emptied the kitchen boxes, I chose a spot to hang my calendar. The dates were cluttered with items needing to be done to accomplish the move and now I set about chronicling the details of setting up life on this end of our journey. I pulled from my experience before of settling into a brand new place. Of finding a new grocery store, a new doctor, a new favorite restaurant.

As I made lists and set about getting things in order, I thought back to a favorite book—*The Accidental Tourist* by Anne Tyler. Being more of a "nester" than a lover of travel, I sympathized with the main character's love of all things familiar, and the feeling of safety that often came with it. Yet his profession as a travel writer often placed him in direct opposition to his nature. Thus, the emblem of his book series emerged: an over-stuffed chair. With wings.

A relationship with a quirky young woman forced him to confront his reluctance to stand up and move out beyond his chair-of-comfort and step forward completely into his exploration.

There was something about this move that made me feel like I was being pushed out of my own soft chair and urged to move forward on the path without my surrounding comforts. My move to California had seemed different—perhaps because I viewed it as temporary or perhaps because I was being drawn forward out of discomfort. It all felt new and exciting.

This move had a completely different tone. While I had my husband and my dog beside me (and certainly much more "stuff") it felt less exciting and a bit more effortful. I had built more equity in life, I suppose, and now it was all coming with me. Into the unknown.

I stared at the dates of the months ahead and I felt compelled to plan them somewhat. Fall was coming and we were excited, after living in an area that experiences only minor season change, to enjoy the deep autumnal colors and more dramatic season changes. But I needed a job and I needed to get settled in some visceral way—to orient myself to where we were and where our family was heading.

Keisha munched on her pork chop as I laid out my plans on my kitchen calendar.

We seemed to adapt well. Within three weeks, I was working at James's new employer doing similar work I had done for the past several years. I continued my yoga practice, moving in and out of the poses on our back patio, under a canopy of pine trees. I missed the sound of the ocean but the stillness of the wooded land and the rich loamy aroma offered a sense of grounded-ness. Keisha watched as I did my daily asanas and kept an eye on the malevolent squirrels hiding in the trees. I found a local mediation group and sat with these new friends as we shared a familiar dance of breath and thoughts.

On the weekends all three of us hopped in the car and explored the area—the North Carolina coast, the Blue Ridge Parkway, the mountains of Asheville. My southern roots luxuriated in the rib-sticking food of biscuits and gravy and fried ham, of slow- cooked greens and pecan pie. The South was reminiscent of my childhood. But James, a native Californian, struggled with the change in climate.

Keisha, as always, rolled with punches.

Our commute to work was long, an hour each way, and Keisha was left at home alone often twelve hours a day. We made sure to secure the garbage lid so no enticement could exist during those long stretches. I was lonely at work, having not yet forged any deep friendships and still feeling a bit unmoored by the difference in topography and even culture. I wished the drive home were not so long so that I could travel there for lunch, like I had done every day in California, to see, hug and kiss my little girl.

When we walked through the door in the evening exhausted after a long day, Keisha greeted us, anxious to see us and go outside. But despite having spent almost twelve hours alone in the house with little to do, she seemed tired. I was concerned that something might be wrong and it would be several months later when I would learn the cause of her fatigue.

For some reason I began to take special note of the progress of time. I had an interesting relationship with time—attached to my calendar and to the forward march of life. Keisha was no longer a young dog but was in her middle years. Each year I celebrated her birthday in August with a cake and candles. We sang. She eyed the cake with anticipation and I sent a silent prayer upward for the blessing that was this incredible being.

I had tucked away that conversation with Jonathan years ago, when I had told him about getting a puppy. Fourteen years. Heartache City. Oh, those words had been planted deep in my brain. But that area of my heart that had been in a painful lockdown those years ago when I first moved to Houston and had been slowly released by the love and presence of Keisha and later James, now felt tight again. Jonathan's words moved from my brain and settled into my heart, where Keisha liked to place her Shavasana bone. I knew that we all are mortal and have limited time here, but as I watched the months and years click by on the calendar I became more aware of the passing of time.

Shortly after we moved to Chapel Hill, we celebrated Keisha's eighth birthday with a white cake and pink roses made of sugar. She looked exactly the same as she had when she was two: her fur was shiny, her eyes sparkled, and she was full of energy. Her body revealed no obvious signs of aging but as Jonathan had reminded me long ago, things don't last forever. Time goes too fast in many ways and, while the birthday celebration marked the gift that *I* had received eight years ago, my fear and paranoia of loss prompted me to find a vet in the area for some reassurance.

As always, she refused the treats offered by the compassionate and gentle vet and resisted all advances of any kind. It appeared her distaste for all things medical had not budged despite the congeniality of the Southern doctor. He listened to her heart and stopped for a moment. His brow furrowed and he listened more intently. My own heart beat fast and furious.

He put down the stethoscope and crossed his arms.

"She may have a bit of a heart murmur," he said, cautiously.

My own heart froze.

"Let's do an X-ray just to take a quick peek." He left the room.

I stared at Keisha whose only reaction was a continued need to escape the confines of this room. I, too, wouldn't mind leaving myself. I did not want to hear anything that might foretell the winding down of my friend's body.

The X-rays were taken and the doctor returned to discuss his findings.

"She does have an enlarged heart," he said.

My stomach turned.

"Does she cough a lot? Has she ever fainted? Does she fatigue easily on walks? Maybe vomited while exercising?"

"Yes," I gulped. "She threw up a couple of time during some long walks."

He must have seen the panic on my face. Her heart—it needed to keep beating. For a long time. Anxiety swept over me.

His own face softened and his voice became soothing.

"There is really nothing to worry about," he offered, trying to calm me. "We'll just monitor it."

But his assurances didn't make me feel any better. I thought of her little heart, beating inside the compact little body. I never wanted it to stop beating. My thoughts were fast and frantic. Stress, I thought, was the heart's enemy! What kind of stress did Keisha have in her life? Squirrels, yes. I'd need to think on solving that one.

Thunderstorms. Oh, the drama of those sent her quivering and panting. That couldn't be good. And now we were living through quite a few that rolled through our area.

I explained Keisha's panting and quivering during intense weather and asked if that might be detrimental to her heart. He looked at me oddly but then considered it for a moment.

"Well, yes. I suppose it could put added stress on her heart."

"What can I do to help with that?" I urged. I needed a plan. Action was required.

He seemed to think for a moment and then reached into the pocket of his white coat. He pulled a pad of paper from the pocket with a pen clipped to the binding.

He scribbled something on the paper, tore it from the pad and handed it to me solemnly.

I read the writing on the prescription form:

Keisha Erickson
Valium 2mg

Take as needed for thunderstorms

I looked up at him confused. He stared back, no hint of expression.

"Seriously?" I thought it might be a joke.

"It could calm her so her nervous system doesn't respond so intensely," he answered.

Well, it was something, I guess, but my fears were responding intensely.

"Doctor, what's the typical life span of a dog Keisha's breed and size?" There—her mortality was now in the room with us.

"Ten to fourteen years is considered normal", he said.

There was that number. That damn number planted deep in brain and in my heart.

We left the office, holding the leash in my one hand and the prescription in the other. I stopped at the local drugstore where the vet had directed us to get the medication filled, and Keisha and I waited on a bench while the druggist plopped the tiny pills into the amber bottle.

The cashier called loudly from behind the register. "Keisha Erickson, your prescription is ready" and we both trotted to the counter. I reached into my purse and handed the clerk my credit card.

"That will be five dollars," she said.

"That's all?"

"Insurance covered it. That's your co-pay," she answered.

Stunned, I returned the card to my wallet and handed her a five dollar bill.

We walked back to the car with our purchase and sat for a moment before heading home.

It had been an odd day, to say the least. I was tempted to reach into Keisha's prescription bottle and take one of those little pills for a test drive myself.

Chapter 30

"I'd just love a Richard Widmark grapefruit to go with my Robert Taylor orange."
— Lucy Ricardo
I Love Lucy

Life had become more routine now in this new land where we lived. And we began to talk about starting a family. I had some trepidation about this next step. I was in my mid-30s and James was close to 40. Among the primary concerns, though, was the often-told tale of a doted-upon dog becoming intolerant of the new family member.

I recalled one of my closest friend's experience when she had her first child: her beloved dog of eight years seemed unable to cope with the addition. Despite all efforts and precautions, the dog had tried to bite the child and had to be moved to a different home. It was heartbreaking. I added that to the bag of fears I toted around.

I often snuggled with Keisha and talked to her about how nice it would be to have another member of the pack. Her dark eyes looked at and watched my lips move. I often wondered how the Doggie Lama perceived these interchanges. I hoped that in whatever way I was communicating, she could somehow understand the importance of what I was talking about.

My beloved calendar now marked my cycles and potential times for conception. It was a roller coaster of hope and disappointment and after several months I got the strong sense that I should take a pregnancy test, long before it was instructed. It was late in the day and I managed to find one last stick in the back of the cabinet. While waiting for the result, Keisha and I took a quick walk along the quiet streets of our neighborhood. Once back at the house I remembered the stick sitting on the counter and, without much hope, I glanced at the results only to find a positive sign.

I was stunned.

I looked at the stick and then at Keisha. She wagged her tail gently back and forth. I think she knew. And she was officially the first one informed.

The happiness lasted until the first violent wave of nausea engulfed me. I had never felt so ill. The morning sickness lasted all day and was at its peak late at night. I moved to the guest room with Keisha as I didn't want to keep James awake. Keisha sat beside me in bed as we munched saltines and watched the *I Love Lucy* reruns that helped take my mind off the churning in my gut. Yes, I, too, loved Lucy Ricardo and I had since I was a child. Lucy was beautiful, stylish and yet her wants and desires often drove her to outlandish pratfalls and mayhem.

"Oh, Ethel, I just HAVE to have one of those grapefruits." And up she scaled Richard Widmark's wall to another disastrous, but comedic, adventure. Poor Ricky, Ethel, and Fred were always mopping up after Lucy's travails, but in the end everyone still loved Lucy.

It always spoke to me as such a comforting statement about our human experience—deep down inside we loved deeply, but often found ourselves in the craziest circumstances, planted there by our own egos and selfish whims. Yet we were still lovable nonetheless.

It now occurred to me, nestled in a pool of saltine crumbs that Keisha was quickly lapping up, that this human experience seemed to cross species. Keisha, too, was beautiful. James and I joked about her healthy self-esteem. She often would pause from her antics and pose just so—her dark fur silky and shiny, her eyes squinting off into the distance. *Feast upon my beauty*, she seemed to say.

At those times, James would lapse into his most perfect Keisha impersonation and quote the Pantene commercial from the 80s: *Don't hate me because I'm beautiful.*

But like Lucy, her poise often fell to her wanton desires. Slap-stick situations resulted from some overwhelming selfish desire, like garbage, hidden snacks or puddles of mud. Like Ricky Ricardo, we picked up the pieces and moved on.

As the black and white images played out on the television screen, Keisha and I digested our midnight snack. Lucy was now hiding herself under a bear skin rug, clutching the grapefruit, in the hopes that Ricky and Richard Widmark would not notice her there.

Lucy was gonna have some splainin' to do.

I had lost ten pounds and had a decidedly green cast to my skin. I could no longer drive to the office and was officially working from home until it had passed. And I prayed it would pass soon. Files were transferred to the house and I began to work from my couch. I had moved my misery out to the living-room sofa, which sat between the front windows overlooking the lawn and the back sliding door with a view of the patio and backyard. From my vantage point on the sofa, I was afforded access to both scenes with only a turn of my head.

Spring was in full riot and the views were magnificently colorful.

It was then that I discovered the source of Keisha's fatigue after a long day at home while we worked.

Keisha began her day at a sentry position at the front window. At some appointed morning hour, the squirrels made their appearance, twitching and taunting the canine occupant staring back at them from the window. She would tremble and growl as she always did, and the squirrels would take their cue and race for the side yard around the back and wait on the deck for more provocation.

As soon as those tiny squirrel paws began their sprint to the back, Keisha, in turn, would pivot on her paws and charge forward toward the backslider.

As the couch (and me on it) stood in direct line of the door, she vaulted over the couch, just lightly using the cushions as leverage, land on the backside of the couch and skid to the glass door where the squirrels were waiting. The jeering and provocations played out again and again. Keisha would tremble and growl in response. The squirrels would turn once again and head back to the front waiting for Keisha's acrobatics to place her at her original sentry position.

My nausea and weakness held me captive on the couch, and I dared not move lest I collide with this force of nature that moved in bursts of power between the front windows and the back. I watched her jump and I ducked, covering my head lest a paw graze my scalp on her arc over the furniture. Her ire and disdain for these creatures were palpable and I could understand why. And I now understood why she was so exhausted each night. This mean-spirited play went on consistently throughout the day with only small respites of napping and water. It seemed like an endless battle and I suspected the squirrels may have organized themselves into regiments and shifts.

It was another Civil War, here in the Deep South. And from the couch, I watched the daily skirmishes.

Chapter 31

*"A squirrel is just a
rat with a cuter outfit."*
— Sarah Jessica Parker

I spent the summer months on that couch during the day while continuing my nights in the guestroom with *Lucy* and crackers. Keisha was beside me the whole way. As the weather cooled and the fall colors began to burn in all their glory, my stomach calmed down and began to grow larger. My own color returned to normal and I headed back to work.

We decided to celebrate my renewed health and our wedding anniversary with a trip to the mountains of Asheville. Keisha was too precious to me, too sensitive a creature to board at a kennel, so she, too, packed her weekend duds and journeyed with us.

Dogs were not allowed in the hotel that we preferred—a stately old stone building that sat atop a hill overlooking breathtaking views. We were relegated to a motel on the interstate that accepted dogs. It was nice, but not plush.

The three of us walked the streets of downtown Asheville, explored parks and Keisha stayed behind at the motel while we toured The Biltmore. It felt good to be able to eat, to feel strong, to explore beyond my front door and to enjoy being with my family.

Our stay had been quick and Sunday morning we packed our bags and were ready to head back home. James and Keisha trekked down the stairs to the car with our bags while I stayed in the room. The door slightly ajar, I was startled by a tremendous explosion of barking and snarling from several dogs in the parking lot. The sounds were violent and filled with emotion and I was concerned for whomever had been involved. Within moments, Keisha burst through the door and jumped across the room to land on the bed. There she plopped her body down and looked at me with an innocent but panting face. Her fur was ruffled, her ears perked but she seemed unscathed.

Not long after, James entered the room looking a bit disgruntled.

"Your dog didn't like the looks of a couple of Dobermans in the parking lot. She gave them the *what-for* and they in turn came back at her with all they had."

The commotion all made sense now.

"Keisha started it, but as always, was not interested in finishing it." The ex-cop was none too pleased.

Keisha was always quick to poke at a sleeping bear, be it a couple of grumpy Dobermans, a spaniel in the park, or a persnickety next-door cat. But once she saw the dangerous ramifications of her impulsivity and pronouncements, she hit the road.

23 Skidoo!

She high-tailed it out of the melee as quick as her paws could carry her. Once she reached some sort of safety, she managed to don a look of complete innocence. Someday she was going to have to deal with what she started.

But today was not that day.

I looked over at her, lounging among the motel pillows. I furrowed my brow and, whether she was reading my body language or my aura, she knew how I felt about this situation. She was a confrontational elitist at times, and it got her into more than one pickle. It was not one of her better traits.

She batted her dark eyelashes, seeing that I was calling her on it. With a lack of any culpability, she glared back at me with her dark, intense eyes.

I did NOT like the riff-raff in the parking lot. I stand by my assessment.

Toward the end of my pregnancy I was put on bedrest and took up residence once again on the couch that provided leverage for Keisha's vaulting antics between the front window and the back slider door. The squirrels, evidently, did not take a break during the winter months.

One Saturday morning while balancing a plate of biscuits and gravy on my belly and devouring the salty, decadent snack, I saw Keisha charge out the sliding door as James opened it to take the garbage out. It was a mere blur of black fur and snarling. She sailed off the back deck in hot pursuit of the enemy and as she landed on the bed of pine needles she emitted a loud cry and stopped dead in her tracks.

James ran to her side. She stood frozen—her back left paw was elevated off the ground and she could not be coaxed to put weight on it, nor to move. James lifted her up and carried her into the house. I sensed the squirrels watching from the lofty heights of the pine trees but heard no heckling. The battlefield was quiet.

Soldier down.

James poked and prodded and Keisha squeaked and snapped at the probing hands. An expensive emergency room visit to the vet revealed that Keisha's leap from the back deck had caused a tendon in her knee to snap. Surgery was required.

Convalescing on the couch that night and waiting for the surgery that would enable her to resume her jaunts, Keisha's dark eyes looked into mine. *I told you those squirrels were evil*, her eyes seemed to say.

Surgery was scheduled for Monday morning, and the estimated cost matched almost exactly the amount of my last paycheck. Having decided to quit work once the baby was born, we had been throwing every penny we had against any outstanding debt. We had succeeded in eliminating it all before we went down to one income and triumphantly placed my last paycheck in our savings account. It seemed its stay there was going to be brief.

Always the proverbial worrier, I sat on the couch that Monday morning, my belly now protruding alarmingly over my thighs, and prayed for a safe and successful operation for my beloved friend. Absent the various medical interventions by Dr. Beck in those early puppy years, this was the first surgery Keisha had ever experienced.

I was distraught.

James returned home that afternoon with the still-drugged dog; her tongue spilled disturbingly out of the side of her droopy face.

"The doc says everything went well. The knee has been repaired and she should be up and active again within a few days or so," James relayed as he tenderly placed the woozy dog in the bed we had fashioned on the living room floor.

"But she looks awful," I said. I had never seen her like this. Pregnant women weren't required to be stoic and I saw no need to try.

"She's fine. She needs to clear the anesthesia from her system."

I looked at the shaved leg and the stitches that marked the surgery site. A brace had been placed on the injured leg.

"They said she'll need to be careful the next few days, and the brace will protect the knee as it heals. And so she doesn't put any weight on it." James's voice was calm and clinical, but I couldn't shake my discomfort at seeing Keisha so vulnerable and lacking her usual vibrancy and resiliency.

I held onto his words the rest of the evening as I stroked her fur, offered bits of kibble and placed her water bowl next to her bed. She acknowledged my nursing efforts with her eyes but remained curled in the bed. The surgery had been an assault to her delicate system. I was not sure if she really was that incapacitated or if her dramatic leanings were playing on my sympathies.

At midnight I made the trek to my bed while Keisha remained sacked out in the living room with James on the couch. She had not moved all night and James offered to stay near. She would hopefully sleep well through the night and things would be better in the morning.

I awakened around 3:00 a.m. with a feeling that something was amiss. I sat up and looked around the room. The house was quiet and nothing seemed out of place. But something in the hallway outside the bedroom caught my eye. I blinked to make out the shape: it was dark and about two feet long, on the floor near my bedroom doorway.

It was Keisha, collapsed on the floor in a pool of urine.

Despite my heavy abdominal load, I sprang from the bed and landed next to my sweet and clearly ailing friend. She looked up at me and her tail thumped against the floor. Her eyes were bright again, the anesthesia must have been clearing. I quickly checked the surgery site—no blood, no tearing. I tenderly probed the leg and the rest of her body for any signs of distress but there didn't appear to be any.

I bent down ever so close to her snoot and asked, "You okay, little one?"

She licked my face with a renewed energy and her tail wagging picked up its tempo. While she and I could not effectively use language to share information, we had honed our communication skills in other ways.

"Did you start feeling better and decide you missed me?" I spoke softly in her ear, so as not to wake James.

Her tail thumped against the floor. The answer was an affirmative.

I got up to get a towel to clean up the mess and when I returned I saw her trying to hoist herself up to follow me. She was still wobbly and the brace was proving too difficult to maneuver.

I settled her back on the floor and mopped up the liquid trailing along the hallway. I did not want to move her lest it jar the stitches, so I grabbed a blanket from the bed and dragged it to where she lay. We would simply camp out here on the floor for the night. She seemed delighted with the decision and I awkwardly maneuvered my round belly to a comfortable position on the floor, with Keisha in front of me. I had to reach over my stomach to stroke her fur. The baby's presence was creating a barrier between me and my dog.

The last few weeks I had thought a lot about the sleepless nights that were part and parcel of having a newborn. My mothering skills would be needed around the clock. Now, it seemed, the call of the night came a few weeks early.

"Soon the baby will be here, Keisha, and we'll be up just like this, in the middle of the night. I guess we can get used to this."

Her eyes watched me in the darkness and I sensed a concern coming from her about the future.

"But nothing changes between you and me. You needed me tonight just like the baby will need me. We are all in this together. We're a family."

I thought how crazy the scene must look to any outsider willing to peek into our bedroom hallway in the wee hours of the morning: an overly large pregnant woman conversing with an injured dog, and snuggling under a rumpled blanket. A mother tending to her little one, discussing family dynamics.

But the discussion seemed vitally important. Keisha sighed deeply and her whole body relaxed. More confirmation of the discussion we were both having. My friend wanted the reassurance that our connection would not change. The mean-spirited squirrel had provided us an opportunity to have this conversation and demonstration of our priorities.

Things felt resolved, there on the floor in the hallway. The next morning Keisha's body was back to its impish vitality and the house seemed more vibrant too. Our conversation had cleared the air and the squirrels eagerly awaited the healthy return of their foe.

My due date, January 3, was approaching quickly and we prepared for the newest member of our family, a boy. He was active and appeared to be growing well. I snuggled with Keisha on the couch and let her be close to the squirming, gyrating baby boy growing inside me. I wanted her to sense that he was part of us. I had no indication if she felt this. She was calm and snuggled with me but offered no confirmation.

I looked at the Christmas tree sitting in front of the window, the lights glowing warmly in the fading sunlight of the room. It was a comforting scene and at that moment, I thought it might be a good time to call Anna and see how things were going on her end. She had given birth to her first child, a girl, about a month earlier. I had only received a quick call from her husband the day she arrived, letting me know that everything had gone smoothly. Maybe things were a bit calmer and I could hear her voice.

"Hello." There it was—my friend's familiar voice.

"I wanted to know how things are going. Are you getting any sleep?" I asked.

"An hour here. An hour there. It's been a blur. But Celeste is beautiful and healthy." I could hear the pride in her voice.

"How's the rest of the household? Drew? Chandon?"

The pause was dramatic.

"Drew is fine." I could hear her breathe in. "Chandon died the day after the baby was born."

I was dumbstruck. I gasped.

Anna was silent.

"My God. Are you all right? What happened?"

She waited for a moment to speak. I could feel her collect her thoughts. She took a breath in.

"He had been having a few symptoms a week before and they were running tests."

I could hear her voice break. She paused.

"It's all so hazy." I could sense the tears were flowing now. "Drew took her in the day after she was born and the vet said it was the best way to proceed."

I didn't want any more details than that. The news had stopped me in my tracks.

We both sat in silence. I was stunned and the tears began to form, stinging and hot. I didn't know what to say.

I heard the soft mewling of the baby on the other end of the phone and pictured Anna holding the squirming bundle. The sound brought me from dark thoughts of death to the new life that was now part of Anna's world. I touched Keisha's fur, thinking of all that we shared, she and I, with Anna and the stoic Chandon. And now he was gone.

"Oh, Anna. I'm so sorry." The words were inadequate. "He was such a great dog, such a wonderful protector." I could see the thick mane of hair ringing his face, his dark eyes. How could my friend bear this?

The tears fell as we talked of Chandon, recounting stories of his adventures, so many with the tiny Keisha running beside him. The memories brought more tears but then we seemed to turn a corner, to revisit all the funny moments. We giggled about his need for cleanliness and order. We laughed about his disgust of the disorder and chaos that Keisha often brought into his world. Dear Chandon.

"It's interesting," Anna noted out loud, "that Chandon left just when Celeste arrived. Life gets turned upside down when a baby arrives. Dirty diapers, round-the-clock-feedings, spit up. Maybe he thought it was all going to be too much," she said, giggling. It was nice that we could share some laughter in the face of such a deep loss.

I laughed with her, but I considered that maybe she had hit on some odd truth. Maybe the timing of it all was not an awful and overwhelming coincidence. Maybe on some level the drastic change in the family was something Chandon was not willing to navigate. He was twelve years old; life had been good. Perhaps the time was right for him to take his leave.

Anna and I talked a bit more, the conversation turning to happier topics of babies and new beginnings. We let the ending be where we had left it. I hung up the phone and looked at Keisha again. She snoozed beside me. Did she know in some intuitive way that her dear friend was gone? Did she sense the impending changes in our family? Would she navigate all of this smoothly or could things play out in the ghastly way that it had in Anna's house? I rubbed my belly and could feel my baby respond. I rubbed Keisha's belly with my other hand and could feel her breath. Her face revealed no answer to my questions. The future was unwritten or at least unknown. I closed my eyes and sent a prayer to whomever was listening. *Please let everything play out in the best way possible.*

I breathed in, held my breath a moment, and let the air from my lungs flow to the space around me.

I added an addendum to my first plea: *And give me the courage and strength to navigate whatever comes my way.*

We spent the next few weeks huddled on the couch, while an early snowfall covered the lawn. Things were going to change very soon.

Chapter 32

"I can't change the direction of the wind, but I can adjust my sails to always reach my destination."

— Jimmy Dean

Two weeks later, I was back on the couch, this time holding Colin, our 8-pound baby boy. I had spent a week in the hospital after his birth. While the delivery had gone well, I had massive hemorrhaging and five hours of emergency surgery had allowed me to stay alive and become a mom. It was all sudden and traumatic, and drained my body in a way that I struggled to understand.

What was to have been only a one-night stay in the hospital stretched to five, and our friend Andrea, who was appointed to feed and check on Keisha, was called in to extend her services. Things had been fine at home, Andrea reported, before the situation took such a dramatic turn. Keisha had welcomed her, eaten, and been taken for a walk. But as the drama unfolded in the hospital, so did events at the house.

My surgery had happened late Monday night and into early Tuesday morning, and Andrea had been called to go over Tuesday morning to feed

Keisha. Keisha met her at the front door with a growl and begrudgingly allowed her in, keeping a good ten-foot distance while food was laid out. She would not allow her leash to be put on, but did go outside for a bathroom break. She quickly skirted inside to resume her stand of the house. She clearly was distraught and wanted only minimal caretaking. Andrea made sure things were safe and continued to check on her twice a day.

The aggressive and protective behavior continued through the week with small respites when James came home for a change of clothes. She was erratic and turned over her water bowl constantly. I lay in the hospital, still reeling from the physical assaults my body had experienced and tried to re-orient myself from that event to caring for my tiny infant. Hearing the news of Keisha's behavior, I was deeply worried. She and I were connected and this was proof. I wanted to comfort her but I didn't know how.

When we finally arrived home, we carefully followed the procedures set out by our vet and others who knew the proper way to mitigate any jealousy on the dog's part toward a new baby. I stayed in the car with Colin while James carried the baby's blanket (and his smell) into the house to introduce him gradually to Keisha. She quickly sniffed it and looked to the front door.

James gave me the signal and Colin and I walked to the house. Keisha's tail feverishly swished back and forth and she followed me to the couch where I sat with Colin on one hip. Keisha sniffed my body intensely, gathering all the information that she could. I kept trying to show her Colin and allow her to smell his unique scent, but she quickly passed over his little wiggling body and was bound and determined to inspect every inch of me.

I handed the baby to James and stretched out on the couch. Keisha jumped up beside me and managed to position herself between the back cushion and my shoulder. Then she did the oddest thing—she scooted next to me and carefully stretched her neck across mine. She had never done anything like this before and I was baffled.

James was watching from the loveseat, where he was cradling Colin.

"It's almost like she's checking my pulse."

I laughed, gently so as not to disturb whatever she was doing, and feeling the warmth of my new fur neck brace.

We stayed like that for a few moments, like two swans entangled at the neck.

But then she moved away from my neck and traveled to the end of the couch where she nestled at my feet. And sighed.

Colin and I were glad to have left the sterile environment of the hospital and be back in the nurturing space of our home. The pack was together again. And safe.

But all was not well.

Our concern about Keisha's acceptance of Colin ended up being wasted energy, or at least so far.

She liked to sleep underneath his cradle. At least until he began to cry, wiggle and eventually wail. Keisha, always the sensitive one, simply took this as her cue to move to a quieter area of the house.

My body had been through too much, it seemed. The long labor and delivery, plus the onslaught of the surgery and drugs had depleted my systems completely. My normal mode of healing, sleep, was not available now, due to a growing baby who needed to be nursed round the clock. And even when I had slots of time where I could sleep, my body would refuse to go into that restorative space.

I dreaded nightfall.

As the world became dark, I looked out our front windows at the neighbors' yards and watched as the lights went on, warm and cozy in the winter chill. As the hours drifted close to midnight, I'd watch them turn off, one by one, as sleep came to each household.

But not mine.

I glared at the dark, silent houses filled with sleeping occupants. Jealously flowed through my body as I longed for that experience again. I was angry that each night everyone around me retreated to the world of sleep and dreams. But I was left alone, awake.

I was tired, I was angry and I was afraid.

My exhausted body craved rest and deep, deep sleep, but it seemed confused and unable to figure out how to do it. I cried. I cried non-stop, as if the tears had an endless source. The world felt heavy and oppressive. My logical mind knew that I was surrounded by blessings and loved ones. And I was finally a mother—the only real goal I had ever had in life. And yet I couldn't touch the joy. I couldn't feel it. It was there, behind a heavy dark curtain.

I'd walk into Colin's nursery and take in the bright colors, the coziness of the room. Stuffed animals smiled back at me from their shelves and the mobile over the crib played the simple melody from Winnie the Pooh as Tigger, Pooh, Piglet and Eeyore floated over the soft bedding. But while my eyes and ears took in the sweetness of the space, my body and my heart could not absorb it.

The sleep that eluded me could have been a respite, a refuge, but it was off limits to my exhausted mind and body.

James and I both grew concerned. I tried gentle walks outside, healthy meals. But nothing seemed to stop the vicious hold this had on me. My physical strength was not returning. I was so weak I thought I might drop my baby as I carried him across the room. My skin was pale with a gray cast and the tears were unrelenting. Smiles and laughter were unavailable. I couldn't even remember what they felt like. I was tired, so very tired.

Finally James placed a call to the doctor.

"She says to go to the emergency room, so you can be admitted." His face was taut with worry.

"No! I don't want to go. I can't leave you guys. You need me." I looked at James, cradling Colin. I did not want to leave my baby, my home. I wanted to get on with this wonderful part of my journey, which was proving to be anything but wonderful.

"Yes, I need you. And Colin needs you. But that's why you need to go. You need to get well."

The events of the last few weeks had pushed my body into something intolerable. But James had endured much, too.

I knew my body needed sleep. Once I could close my eyes and withdraw into that restorative place, my body could find the strength to sort out the disorganization that flowed through it. That was the tonic I knew my body craved. So at 10:00 o'clock that night we packed a bag and headed out into the cold toward the hospital. We wound our way through the emergency room admittance. I answered question after question of what was happening. Yes, I knew my name. Yes, I knew what day it was. January 25, 1998. The Broncos had just won the Super Bowl that night. We had watched it in our living room.

Colin was with us as we had no one to watch him and he needed to eat. Keisha was at home standing guard.

By 2:30 a.m. I was checked into Room #431—the room where I would hopefully get well. The room where I could rest and heal and dismantle this wall that stood between me and all the great things in my life. I wanted to touch them, kiss them, hug them, and even smell them.

But I couldn't do any of those things.

I couldn't get to anything beyond this burden of heaviness and sleeplessness.

The only thing my body recognized was thickness, sadness, mind-numbing fatigue and the inability to escape into sleep.

At that moment an odd memory from college emerged out of nowhere: reading Jean Paul Sartre's

No Exit for a philosophy class. I remembered how the main characters discovered themselves in hell—a bright room which contained no exit. There was no respite from the room, from the light, from anything. And most especially from themselves. They were frantic to physically escape the room, but also to flee the situation at any level—but there was no sleep, no ability to close their eyes, not even the ability to blink, as if toothpicks propped the lids open. The image had struck me at the time and now came forth from somewhere deep in my brain.

I reached up and covered my eyes. I blinked. No toothpicks.

I closed my eyes. But sleep eluded me.

My room was quiet as all the other occupants on the floor seemed to be doing the thing I could not do; I was surrounded by those who had access to that blissful state. I had kissed James and Colin goodbye and they were headed home to rest. James knew that he would have to use the formula in the cupboard for Colin's next feeding if the breastmilk I had pumped ran out. Hopefully, my little cottage with Colin, James, and Keisha was quiet by now, and they were safe and sleeping. But here I was exhausted, confused, and near another flood of tears.

I was a new mother. I had a job to do. I had never felt such responsibility before as caring for this tiny human being. And yet my body had betrayed me. I reluctantly came to the hospital, as it seemed to be the only avenue that might right me and get me back to my family and new maternal role. I sat on the edge of the bed and looked at my reflection in the window that was dark with the cold January night. I saw the closed door behind me with my jacket hanging from a silver hook. I contemplated the parade of fears that marched in front of me. My baby was going to spend his first night away from his mom. We had not been apart for over nine months, cocooned next to each other, sharing our blood.

Would he take milk from his bottle? Would James be able to take care of him? He had never done anything like this before. Would Keisha revert to her aggressive behavior amidst all the turmoil? Would I ever emerge from this cloak of sadness and experience the simple sweetness of sleep?

I was overwhelmed with the weight of the questions. My head dropped to my chin and the tears started to flow. They fell in rivulets onto my hospital gown, the tears staining the blue and white fabric with splotches of darkness. I could not, nor did I want them to stop. As I looked down through the tears, I noticed my bare feet on the hospital tile floor. They looked odd. They didn't look like my feet at all. They looked puffy and my toes didn't have the same curve they normally did. They were different.

And so was I.

I was now a mother and I didn't have access, or so it seemed, to anything that could help get me back on those feet and move forward. I looked again at my reflection in the window. Who was the person staring back at me? All at once I longed for the past. Before I was married and before I was a mother with a child to raise.

I wanted to be free again. I wanted to feel all the wonderful things I felt then. And, oh, I wanted Keisha beside me. I wanted to walk these feet to wherever she was, invite her into my little sports car, where she and I spent so many hours. I wanted to drive with her at my side, anywhere. Anywhere but here. It was all too much. I needed to be free from all this and to feel her sweet innocent presence. I smiled when I pictured my fantasy. I could feel the movement of the car, the feel of the wind and the presence of my best friend beside me. It gave me relief—something that had eluded me the last few weeks.

No exit.

The only exit I had at this point was an imaginary outing with my best friend at my side.

I laid down on the bed and stared at the ceiling. I pulled the blanket over me and nestled it under my chin. It smelled like this place of tile floors, fluorescent lights and muffled nurse's voices.

I closed my eyes and somehow, miraculously, I drifted off to sleep.

Chapter 33

*"Set wide the window.
Let me drink the day."*
— Edith Wharton,
Artemis to Actaeon and Other Verses

Somehow those few days in the hospital allowed my body to find its center again. I was allowed to have Colin and James visit twice a day. Yes, they had done fine the first night. Colin had slept six hours straight. Keisha was fine. She stayed close to Colin most of the time.

One-by-one, my fears were proven as unwelcome fantasy, and the weight on my shoulders lifted. I slept for long stretches when I was able. Being in a teaching hospital, medical students paraded through my room at all hours and observed me like a lab rat in its cage. They discussed my case among themselves as if I couldn't hear them. They speculated and made judgments about me as if I no longer qualified as a human being.

This lab rat now had some sleep under her belt. My body and my brain were finding their footing and my strength was returning. I felt a new resiliency emerging from this harrowing experience.

On my second morning there, I was awakened from the inkiness of a deep and heavy sleep as the group of interns noisily shuffled into my room, jolting me from my body's much needed, restorative work. I looked at the clock on the wall: 7:00 a.m.

"You've poked and prodded me enough," I barked. Perhaps my need to people-please had been depleted right along with my blood volume.

Clutching their clipboards to their chest, they stared at the lab rat and turned to the lead doctor, looking to him to deal with the surly specimen.

"Mrs. Erickson," the doctor said in a gentle but condescending voice. "We are just here to check on you."

"It's 7:00 a.m." I glared at the group of eyes all staring at me in my flimsy hospital gown. "If you check my chart, you should see what my body has endured the last few weeks." I went on, "And you'll also see in the notes that I've told everyone that the most important thing I need at this point is SLEEP. I know my body well, and once I get access to that, I can and will heal. I was deep in sleep until everyone barged in here."

At least I didn't growl and threaten to nip, like someone I knew.

Each one looked down at their clipboards, shuffled their notes and some even jotted some words onto the page. God only knew what they were writing.

But I didn't care. My surge of anger had tired me and I lay back against the pillows while they whispered amongst themselves.

"We are very glad you are doing better, Mrs. Erickson," the lead doctor said. And with that they shuffled out of the room. Two days later the sleep had allowed me to find space above the wall of sadness for longer and longer stretches of time. The body was an amazing machine.

I left the hospital for a second time and joined my family.

My little household had banded together and survived their own test. All three had been taking walks in the neighborhood while I was gone and had ventured out in the car for a nice drive. Colin quickly slipped into a deep sleep with the movement of the car, and Keisha immersed herself in the sights and sounds of the fast moving scenery. They were two contented member of the household, it appeared.

We were surviving, and we might actually begin to thrive.

I continued to heal and regain my strength. Colin grew fatter and smiled often.

Shortly after Colin's second month of life, James received a job offer back in California, only one mile from our old condo. I peered outside the window to the towering pine trees: they had sheltered us from the intense summer sun and offered a canopy to the winter snowfall as well. But I longed for that golden sunlight of California and my being craved the blue Pacific. Having just had a baby, I was in full nesting mode, but after the trauma of the birth and the subsequent struggles, my homing device called back to the place that had offered me sanctuary years before.

So as the spring bulbs began to poke through the earth in our front yard, we once again packed our belongings (our newest occupant having an extraordinary amount of accoutrements) and headed west. Keisha once again had her belongings in the plastic grocery sack, and she eagerly hopped in the car. But with the changes in the pack, she took up a different spot in the car. Colin and I were loaded into the backseat together with the diaper bag while Keisha had now been promoted to the front seat, riding shotgun with her beloved James.

She virtually beamed with delight. She sat straight up in the seat looking forward as our car retraced its steps along the interstate heading west. I sat in the backseat and chuckled. We had arrived less than two years ago, the three of us. And now Colin was here, and we were heading back. Somehow we needed to come east to get him and then we were free to return.

The travelers did well on the long journey back. Colin and I slept for long stretches while Keisha and James kept vigil in the front. Never again would I take sleep for granted! I took advantage of the lengthy hours in the car and snoozed through the miles.

My spirit had turned the corner to healing at that moment in the hospital when I visualized my drive to freedom with Keisha, and now my spirits felt the healing almost complete as our car turned onto Highway 101 which hugged the coastline of San Diego. We drove alongside the waves and sand, and opened the windows to let the salty air swirl through the car.

Keisha's fur danced in the wind.

We were home.

Chapter 34

"The nitrogen in our DNA, the calcium in our teeth, the iron in our blood, the carbon in our apple pies were made in the interior of collapsing stars. We are all made of starstuff."

— Carl Sagan
Cosmos

We were getting used to packing and unpacking; we had a lot of practice lately. While the physical objects of our life were being pulled from boxes and put in their new home, I noticed I was unpacking the same worries and fears that had plagued me too often.

Wherever you go, there you are.

While I was not playing Russian roulette with my checkbook like I did when I was single and living in Houston, I still held my breath each time I wrote a check or swiped my credit card. Two incomes in North Carolina went a long way while one income in California, not so much.

My little sports car needed to be sold. The baby carrier wouldn't fit. I needed a new car.

The real estate market was bustling, and prices were soaring by the minute. Not long after I had unpacked all the boxes in our rented house, we decided it was best to catch the wave of the latest real estate surge and jump in or we might never be able to swim in the emerging market.

We found a two-story, Mediterranean-style home, complete with deep-fuchsia-colored bougainvillea spilling onto its red clay roof. Contracts were drawn up with a sales price that made me gulp, and hundreds of pages of mortgage papers were signed and notarized. Finally we were handed the keys in exchange for the promise of writing a too-large check, in my opinion, to the mortgage company every month.

Another reason to gulp.

We took extra care to study the health of our retirement accounts. Would there be enough to take care of us? We were parents now. We needed to have wills drawn up. We needed to appoint guardians for Colin should something happen to us.

I thought back to the worries and fears of my twenties that had eroded my peace of mind. I had a whole new set of worries now and they, too, gnawed at my happiness. But at every point of life, I learned that there's always something to worry over or fear. The stakes just seemed higher now.

Keisha, on the other hand, settled in with little concern about the future. Squirrels had been left behind on the East Coast, and I suspected she may have given a certain gesture to the varmints as she bid them adieu. She adjusted quickly to the new environment and our new schedule. Walks in the neighborhood afforded her the opportunity to determine potential new friends as well as decided dislikes. The black Lab down the street, Baxter, was not one to be tolerated. Growls and barks met his tail-wagging greeting. The striped Tabby, Chloe, across the street: not be to be trusted. The Cockapoo next door, Dini, was annoying. She was coolly ignored. The dachshund that lived two streets over could be endured.

But across the street lived a wonderful new friend of Keisha's. We encountered Rita one evening as we returned home from a long walk. She was in her mid-eighties, with snow white hair pulled up into an elegant French knot. Her blue eyes were striking with kohl black liner accentuating their size and shape.

"Well, hello there!" she exclaimed in her Trans-Atlantic accent, waving a graceful, manicured hand towards us. Keisha pulled me and the leash toward the woman standing on the curb. "Who are YOU?" She smiled as she bent down, and Keisha jumped into her waiting arms. It appeared to be love at first sight.

Rita, I was to learn, had been an actress in Hollywood in the forties and fifties. "I was in the picture business," she explained. She had been under contract to some of the major studios at the time: Columbia, MGM, RKO.

Keisha had always enjoyed a flair for the dramatic, and it appeared that kindred spirits were uniting. What a pair these two were going to be. Their chemistry was instantaneous and I felt a bit like a third wheel.

I listened to Rita's stories about the Golden Age of Hollywood with great interest, but I noticed that the most entertaining exchanges happened between those two. Rita petted and kissed Keisha amidst the flourish of her great stories and Keisha nestled into the film star's body, smiling and wagging her tail and enjoying whatever yarn Rita was serving up that day.

Keisha had wasted no time settling into the neighborhood.

Colin was growing every day, and Keisha became more and more interested in the newest pack member. Her cold nose and wet tongue made Colin giggle and the giggle, in turn, made Keisha's tail wag harder.

A deep and abiding friendship occurred once Colin began solid food. He quickly learned the fun of tossing food to the floor and watching Keisha quickly slurp it up. She would look up, tail swishing, lips smacking and wait for another toss. Colin would laugh a deep chortle at the show, his blond hair tousled over his forehead and his cheeks crimson from the laughter.

We returned to all of our old daily staples. It felt comforting to shop at the local Von's, to go to our favorite Italian restaurant, and to resume Keisha's checkups with her old vet. My vigilance over her aging process was never far from my consciousness, and I was apprehensive as we entered her annual appointment. She was now ten years old.

I continued being drawn to studies of the Eastern traditions, especially of India, as my yoga studies included saints and masters from that exotic region of the world. I loved the rich colors of the culture, the deep magentas, spicy oranges, cerulean blues. We often had dinner at the Indian restaurant down the street and we tucked into the equally vibrant flavors of the curries and rice dishes. The wife of the owner often waited on our table, and she wore the traditional garb of her native land. Her saris were shiny with the tightly woven silk, dyed with intense color, and the fabric draped in soft folds across her tiny body. She also wore a *bindi*, a red dot placed between the eyebrows, commonly worn by Hindu women.

I was familiar with the *bindi* and knew its location coincided with the area in meditation where we were instructed to bring our focus—the third eye, the seat of consciousness. I found it interesting that this same spot was where I kissed Keisha each day as I left for work or whenever I was leaving her at home. Or should say I TRIED to kiss. She displayed her disapproval of my action by turning away from me, defiantly rejecting my display of love. But I held fast, tightened my grip around her furry ears and planted a sloppy kiss on her third eye, where the Indian culture places the *bindi*.

But it seemed that Keisha did have her own dot of some sort. It wasn't on her forehead, though.

Keisha's resistance and determination to escape anything that involved grooming or medical probing was now legendary. We most often were greeted by employees of these establishments with a tight grin, a steeling of the eyes, and girding of their loins. They all knew that business with this customer was not easy, was usually very loud and might involve pulled muscles. At our next vet visit, as Keisha and I waited in the examining room for the doctor to appear, I glanced at her file on the metal table.

A plump red dot sat beside her name, on the tab of the file folder. There were other patient files sitting atop the cabinet, and I checked the tab of each name noticing that none of them had any sort of dot. Whatever the vibrant red circle was meant to communicate did not seem cheery. As the doctor entered the room, his jaw braced. Keisha pulled with a Herculean force toward the exit and dragged me out of my seat.

"Good morning, Keisha," the vet said, in much the same way Patton must have greeted a German general.

And the usual melee ensued. Snarls, snaps, wrestling on the metal table. As we mercifully wrapped up the visit, I somehow managed to remember the issue of the red dot.

"If you don't mind my asking," I queried, "is there some significance to the red dot on Keisha's file?"

My stomach churned a bit.

"Oh," he said, a bit caught off guard but not bothered by the question. "It means 'WILL BITE'. It's a warning to the staff."

At that he handed me our paperwork and quickly exited the room.

Holding the papers in one hand and her leash in the other, I looked down at Keisha, who seemed equally relieved to part ways from the man in the white coat. She looked up at me and smiled. Her tongue fell out of her mouth and to the right. She cocked her head to one side.

There was a perceptible twinkle in her eyes. I had the oddest sensation that it had something to do with that bright red dot, Keisha's *bindi*, and a bit of pride.

Our family of four had been in their new base of operations on the West Coast for more than a year and had resumed the forward progress of life. Colin grew and flourished, James burrowed into an intense and demanding job, and Keisha appeared grateful for the respite from squirrels and tended to the smallest member of our family in sweet ways. Having no demonstrable maternal instincts prior to Colin, Keisha watched him in a silent, protective way, and she never once attempted to snatch food from his tiny hands—surely a chore of indescribable restraint.

I adjusted to being a stay-at-home mother. The transition, one I thought would be simple, was not necessarily easy. I had honed my skills of focus and commitment in the corporate world. And I was rewarded for it—in glowing annual reviews and monetary compensation. My new job and my new employer operated in a much different way with long hours, constantly shifting demands and little praise or accolades.

But the rewards were greater, of course.

Our stay in North Carolina had kept Keisha from our usual contact with the ocean and prior to that our trips to the beach usually involved walking along the sand on a leash or driving beside the ocean. But now we made frequent trips to Dog Beach where leashes were cast aside, and dogs were left to express their joy in whatever way possible.

A sign at the entrance to Disneyland reads: *Happiest Place on Earth* but I suspected that the sign must have been moved from its original location: the designated Dog Beach. I had witnessed no more intense concentration of cavorting and frolicking than on that section of coastline. Both Keisha and Colin loved the beach, and we often journeyed to Del Mar to join the four-legged fun in the surf and sand.

As I watched, with more than a little bit of voyeurism, the play and sheer delight of those beachgoers, I reflexively smiled. I thought back to the afternoon in Houston as I responded the same way to seeing Keisha romp in the carpet padding she had dislodged from the apartment. There was something about the unabashed bliss of a dog that sparked something deep within me. It bubbled up through my heart, up my throat and spread to my mouth in a full, delicious smile.

I savored the feeling and sent another prayer of thanks for the gift of dog.

And most especially for the gift of Keisha.

Most nights found us in the same routine. Colin slept in his nursery down the hall and the three remaining members of the pack congregated on the king-sized bed of the master bedroom.

I lounged on the left with a pile of books on my nightstand: *Autobiography of a Yogi. The Yoga Sutras of Patanjali. Hatha Yoga Pradipika. The Bhagavad Gita.* James sat propped with his array of pillows, his own nightstand laden with books of his choosing: *The Elegant Universe. In Search of Schrödinger's Cat. A Brief History of Time.* Keisha placed herself in the trough of blankets and pillows in the middle. Her entertainment was chewing on the yellow plastic toy rolled to resemble a newspaper: *The Daily Growl.* Her rubber pork chop had been replaced several years before.

As I consumed the ancient rishis' exploration into the nature of the universe, James immersed himself in the world of physics. His passion for this topic had been around since he was a teenager and I often teased him about seeking out such lofty and laden topics for an evening wind-down. But then again my reading could not be considered light, either. We were, on many levels, nerdy and a good match.

I glanced at the book atop the pile on my nightstand—*Man's Eternal Quest.* Weren't most of us looking for the deeper meaning of life? I remembered the stirrings of that curiosity as a child. Each Sunday morning I watched with admiration as my mother donned her finest dress, reached into her jewelry box sitting atop the dresser, and chose whichever sparkly earrings and necklace would add the final touch. My father, dressed in a dark suit and starched white shirt, held his well-worn bible. I felt great pride as we walked into the cavernous church each week, my beautiful mother gazing up to the altar and singing with her soprano voice these songs that were written for God's ears. But I was listening, too.

I followed my parents' gaze to the altar, with its soaring wood columns and the rich velvet drapes behind the suspended cross. It spoke of the mystery of something great, beyond the building with the stained-glass windows and the burning incense. I watched them as they immersed themselves in devotion to this mysterious and elusive force. I wanted to understand it. To see it. To feel it.

Thirty something years later, the search continued. My husband and I both sought some sort of context to understand where our experiences of life, our small portion of this earthly existence, fit into the greater scheme of things, of the cosmos. Like many, we both longed for a deeper understanding. I chuckled at the disparity of our piles of books, and yet on closer examination they seemed to speak of the same questions and truths.

Long before scientists and physicists of the 20th century began to explore the deeper nature of our universe, the space between the particles and the laws that informed our physical world, the ancient yogis delved into the same search. While present-day physics sought to explain the unseen and the unknown of our vast universe, the yogic texts revealed the concept of *maya* or the cosmic delusion, which divides, measures out, the *Unidentified Infinite* into the finite forms and forces.

The physical world, they told us, was a play of light and energy and as humans we experienced the complex world through our limited perceptions. Yoga instructed us in perceiving beyond our restricted human perceptions to the underlying structure of our universe. We could move beyond our limited understanding and beliefs to a clearer idea of our role in the grid of existence.

While the yogis donned their dhoti cloths and explored the universe from the lotus position, moving beyond the limits of their minds and the five senses, Post-Newtonian scientists and physicists did their work wearing lab coats, using accelerometers, vacuum tubes, and lasers.

I pulled one of my favorite books onto my lap and flipped through the well-worn pages. Paramahansa Yogananda's *Autobiography of a Yogi* was considered a classic and addressed the congruence of the two disciplines.

I read out loud to James.

"'*The stream of knowledge,*' Sir James Jeans writes in *The Mysterious Universe, 'is heading toward a non-mechanical reality; the universe begins to look more like a great thought than like a great machine. Twentieth-century science is thus sounding like a page from the {ancient} Vedas. From science, then, if it must be so, let men learn the philosophic truth that there is no material universe; its warp and woof is* maya, *illusion.*'"

His eyebrows shot up and he reached over to his pile of books and spent a few minutes looking through several.

"Here," he said, flipping through one of his favorite books. "'...*everything we call real is made of things that cannot be regarded as real. If quantum mechanics hasn't profoundly shocked you, you haven't understood it.*'"

"Who said that?" I wondered.

"Niels Bohr. Here's another one..." He flipped through another book, resting on a dog-eared page. "'*After the conversation about Indian philosophy, some of the ideas of Quantum Physics that had seemed crazy suddenly made much more sense.*' That's from Werner Heisenberg."

Neither of those names meant anything to me but we were at it again—dueling banjos (or sitars) of yoga and physics.

"What's that quote I love so much?" James always seemed to catch the out-of-left field-ers I often pitched his way.

He knew immediately. "'*The first gulp from the glass of natural sciences will turn you into an atheist, but at the bottom of the glass God is waiting for you.*' That's Heisenberg, too. He won a Nobel in Physics in the '30s."

Smart guy, I thought.

James had explained that quantum physics was beginning to reveal how the conscious mind not only observed the physical universe but was in fact an active participant in determining how our world unfolded. The observer, scientists were finding, actually influenced the outcome of an experiment with their consciousness through the act of observation, as well as their beliefs or expectations.

I thought back to my art classes, shifting my perceptions, and to all the books I had read during my month-long hiatus from work all those years ago. *Thoughts were things*, they said, *use them to create.*

Scientists were now seeing what the mystics and artists had known all along: we are creative influencers in a universe that extends far beyond our fixed perceptions. Einstein said "Reality is merely an illusion albeit a persistent one." Things may not always be what they seem.

So as James and I explored the cosmos from either side of the bed, Keisha continued her conversation with *The Daily Growl*. Holding my book on my chest, I watched her and thought back to that first awareness of Keisha's possible deeper perceptions—her barking at my meditation. Was Rama correct? Was she perceiving the energy in and around my physical body? Was Keisha indeed a wayward Tibetan Lama who was now manifesting in the form of a mischievous but loving dog?

Five years ago those questions would have seemed preposterous, if not laughable, to me. But those piles of books on our nightstands reminded us that our world and the universe beyond held many mysteries and truths that 100 years ago would be considered implausible or even magic.

Keisha sighed and rolled on her back. She stretched her legs up into the air and the energy moved out through her paws, claws splaying in a wide stretch. She rolled back to her tummy and settled in to sleep.

Maybe we were overthinking all of this. Maybe the answers to the universe were wrapped in the plastic cylinder of *The Daily Growl*. Maybe the bumper sticker *Dog is God spelled backwards* was a big hint from the universe. Life's greatest wisdoms could often be found plastered on the rear end of a car. If God is Love then that's a pretty good description of a dog.

Were dogs some easily accessible experience of our true nature? Was Keisha more in tune to the mysteries of life than us mere humans? Were dogs emissaries from The Almighty?

So many questions.

Maybe, I thought, Keisha was living the answers.

Chapter 35

"All you need is faith, trust and little bit of pixie dust."
— Peter Pan

I hated change. A few times in my life I welcomed change with open arms. My move to the West Coast was a welcome and needed change. But for the most part, I resisted. I complained. I bargained. I resisted some more.

But change is a constant. Colin was teaching me that. Just when we'd managed to master one thing (like sprouting new teeth, or rolling over or crawling) we were on to the next: walking, running, climbing, talking, and learning to say NO! His little body grew and changed so rapidly, he was essentially a different person every few months. It took my breath away sometimes.

Yes, life was about the journey but I still just wanted to get to a nice place, sit down and enjoy the view for a while.

My years in the corporate world had offered a bit more consistency. Numbers were numbers. Spreadsheets were appallingly similar. Monotonous meetings. Legal review of contracts. It was all pretty similar. My little cubicle, with its dull brown fabric walls, boxed me in day after day.

But that part of my life seemed to be over for now. I was a wife. I was a mom. I was a homeowner. No meetings. No conference calls. No memos.

I had more free time and that posed a problem: I had more time to think. My almost-forty years here on the planet had taught me that being alone with my thoughts was often dangerous and at the very least anxiety-provoking. I had no desire to step back into the corporate world. My job had always been that– just a job. I enjoyed my relationships there but my identity was always forged outside the office.

Moving from two incomes to one had stretched my creative skills in more ways than one. Our enjoyment of dining out was too expensive, so I stepped into the kitchen each night to try and cobble a palatable meal together.

Travel was limited, just day trips usually.

The house was still sparse with furnishings, and the walls were alarmingly bare. I tried to channel my busy, often worry-prone mind with distractions. Creative endeavors were often the solution.

I pulled out the small sewing machine my mom had gifted me a few years back ("you might need it," she offered) and began cutting and sewing curtains for the house. I pushed Colin's stroller through the aisles of fabric stores, fingering the heavy drapery fabrics and admiring the rich colors and intricate patterns.

I sat at the kitchen table with my sewing machine, Keisha sleeping beneath the table and Colin munching his snack while I learned to line drapes, make pillows and use fabric in any way I could. The drapery fabric would puddle and fall around Keisha. She didn't try and move away. Rather, she liked being in the thick of things.

One afternoon while Colin and Keisha played with a pile of toys on the floor of the nursery, I pushed Colin's crib away from the wall and began to sketch some drawings from his favorite movie, Peter Pan. We actually owned the walls now (or at least were co-owners with the bank) and I was allowed to alter them in whatever way I chose.

I grabbed a charcoal pencil and sketched the pirate ship where Captain Hook and Mr. Smee sailed the seas. I was drawing on the walls! I felt like a child doing something naughty, and it made my skin tingle. I moved to another space on the wall, and drew a dolphin leaping above the waves. A few feet further along the wall, a whale spewed water from his blow hole. I sketched the shore where a lighthouse stood majestically facing the waves, its lights trying to reach the wooden sailing ship and its black and white stripes swirled to the top.

I penciled in craggy rocks where mermaids sat, winking at the toddler in the room. Before I knew it I had covered two contiguous walls, from floor to ceiling with a Peter-Pan-themed seascape.

I completely lost track of time; my thoughts were totally absorbed in drawing. The sea creatures looked at me, smiling from their positions in the blue ocean. I turned to my companions that had been watching me and smiled. They both smiled back at me, not sure why I was so pleased but knowing it was a good thing.

The next day the three of us trudged to the hardware store to purchase paints to bring color to the charcoal drawings. A gallon of deep blue was chosen along with a pint of white. The blue would cover a third of the wall space as the ocean. I could lighten the rest with the white paint for the sky.

We traipsed home with paints and paintbrushes and as soon as Colin was napping, Keisha and I stepped into my new "art studio". She watched me pour and mix the paints. Her eyes followed me as I rolled on the huge swaths of blues while tiny droplets of paint spray from the foam roller nested in her black fur. She didn't seem to mind.

Never having painted anything so big before, I was a bit nervous. But as my friend's dark eyes watched over me, I again lost myself in a world of paint, color and imagination. I was used to drawing and painting within the confines of a canvas, usually no larger than a few feet, compressing my drawing to fit the space. But now my sense of perspective needed to stretch nine feet high and span twenty or more feet of wall space. I extended and reached, covering the expansive canvas with my creation. It was so large I could almost step into it. I was creating another world. Or at least one that stretched along two walls of a toddler's bedroom.

I purchased craft paints to fill in the whale, dolphins, ship and mermaids. I feathered in glitter among the waves, so that the light could sparkle along the crests of the water to mimic the glistening of the waves that I found so hypnotic at the beach.

I painted a brown, sandy shore along the baseboards and glued touches of sand and seashells to the wall so Colin could touch them. One afternoon after his nap I pulled his socks off, dipped the soles of his feet in a darker brown paint and "walked" his painted feet along the shoreline, creating foot prints along the beach. He giggled and wiggled his toes.

Keisha watched silently at the odd scene in front of her. I paused, considering for a moment if I might like to add some dog prints in the "sand" as well.

"What do you think, Little Miss?" I asked her. She blinked.

Nope, I reasoned, Keisha's paws were notoriously sensitive. Many times I tried to hold her paws, stroke or even kiss them. But the display of affection was always met with a raucous response. She nipped at my fingers and pulled away like a bucking bronco. *Don't touch the paws*, she warned.

I had an idea, though. I wanted Keisha to be included in the scene. I grabbed a paint brush and dipped it into a small bottle of black paint. I crouched at the corner of the wall near the door. There, in the tiny space, I quickly painted the cartoon of Keisha that I had crafted through the years: tipped ears, long snoot, back paws tucked beneath her belly. A swishing tail. It was only about four inches in size but it was there: a tiny Easter-egg for anyone to find as they enjoyed the ocean.

Maybe now that I had some life under my belt, and spent my days and nights with two companions who were aficionados of play, I too could learn how to have some fun!

While Colin's room was cluttered with paints, brushes and plastic sheets as my creative juices flowed, he began spending nights with me in the big bed in the master bedroom. I was glad for the extra company. James's work was keeping him in the San Fernando Valley, one hundred miles away, during the week. He left at 5:00 a.m. on Monday morning and didn't return until 8:00 o'clock on Friday night. The weekdays were lonely and the evenings quiet.

One Wednesday night I couldn't sleep. Colin snuggled beside me curled next to his stuffed animal, Cosmo, fast asleep while Keisha lounged between us. Her breathing pattern indicated she was deep in sleep, as well. I lay in the pool of the light from the bedside lamp, wide awake, magazines strewn around me.

I looked at the clock on my bedside stand. The blue, gleaming numbers silently announced 1:39 a.m. The house was quiet and dark. Rolling onto my side, I reached my hand to Keisha's back, rubbing the silky fur. It had been twelve years since that first night she came to live with me. She had demanded to snuggle with me in the comfort of my blankets and pillows. And things had not changed since then.

I turned out the light and settled back into my pillow when a noise caught my attention. I kept still and listened for it again. There, in the side yard, underneath the bedroom window I heard another faint noise. At that moment, the motion-activated light perched above the side yard door to the garage turned on, illuminating the window near my bed and brightening the dark room.

My heart began to beat faster.

Keisha's head shot up, ears perked. She emitted a low growl. Colin continued to sleep.

Keisha's growling stopped as she became very still, intently searching the environment for another noise. My own ears were straining to detect any other disturbance to the heavy quiet of the night. It was hard to hear anything as my ears were still ringing from the low growl that had pierced the silence.

I slowly got out of the warm bed and headed for the stairs. Keisha jumped into action and sailed past me, turning the corner at the bedroom door, heading down the stairs, two at a time. I followed her down the dark stairwell and into the kitchen. She led me past the kitchen island, through the breakfast nook to the glass French doors overlooking the back patio. At that moment she burst into ferocious snarls and barks, crouching on her back paws and putting her snoot low and to the ground. The hair stood up on the back of her neck. She bared her white teeth.

Something or someone was on the patio.

My heart was pounding and Keisha's loud recriminations were deafening. I leaned to my right to try and see what Keisha was responding to, cautious that I might be detected through the glass. My breath caught as I saw the face of the culprit. His eyes were dark, menacing and looking for a fight.

The fat, surly raccoon stared brazenly at the barking dog. He had no intention of fleeing and stood his ground as if to taunt the now very disturbed Keisha.

Relief flooded through me as I tried to shake off the adrenalin that had pumped through my veins the last few moments.

"Keisha! It's okay," I said. The growls, barks and pleas to open the door continued. I walked back into the kitchen, pried the junk drawer open. The drawer had been caught by the hammer stuffed among the gazillion items living there. I vowed to organize it tomorrow as I dug through the contents and located a flashlight.

Walking back to the glass doors, I clicked the light on and shined it directly in the eyes of the dark bandit. I had to give him credit. He stood his ground, insolent and unrepentant for trespassing. Keisha continued her tirade.

I picked up my brave and loyal watch dog and carried her up the stairs. She continued to growl but she seemed to understand the trespasser had been given a reprieve. Colin was still sleeping, despite the ruckus, and I plopped Keisha down between him and me. Pulling the covers up to my chest, I settled back into my nest and took a breath.

The incident had only taken a few moments to play out but it would probably be a while before I might be calm enough to hope for sleep. Keisha didn't seem to have that problem. She was already curled up, snoot to tail.

As I lounged beside my peaceful companions, I thought back to that night so long ago in Houston when my sleep had been broken by the sound of someone at my door. That heart-racing moment had led me to Keisha, now snuggled next to me. She was to be my protector from that moment on. Tonight she had done a great job.

I thought back not only to that night but to my life at that moment. My little apartment. My money woes. My job frustrations. My cautious heart. My uncertainty of where life was taking me, where my place in the world might be.

Fast forward all those years. So much had changed. The night noises of urban Houston were replaced by the quiet evenings of suburban San Diego. My tiny apartment on Lake Street, with its brown shag carpet and college dorm décor, was a distant memory. The space I now shared with three of my favorite beings on earth was slowly becoming a real home, with home-made curtains, scattered toys and Disney characters on the walls.

I hadn't seen a spreadsheet in several years. My current job only required a full and available heart: being a wife and a mother. My heart had mended through the years. I had no idea where *he* was. The miles between Texas and California had put physical distance between us, and our sparse communications had dwindled to silence. We had gone our separate ways. I wondered where his path had led him.

It was eye-opening to compare two scenes of life, distant in time, but strung together by a moment of awareness and perspective. A dramatic transformation had occurred yet consisted of a string of incremental changes, like a strand of pearls, sometimes moving back upon itself before continuing its forward march.

I moved to bring my face close to Keisha's snoot. Her black fur made her hard to see in the darkness. It felt cozy here, in the softness of the blankets. She opened her eyes and looked at me. I felt a wave of love for my dear friend. She had been witness to and participated in every step during those changes. And she had never lost sight of her first task: to keep me safe.

Tonight she had been ready to save me from a portly, obstinate raccoon. And I had the impetus to finally clean out the junk drawer in the kitchen.

Chapter 36

"I dream of a better tomorrow, where chickens can cross the road without being questioned about their motives."
— Unknown

Motherhood felt like an all-consuming endeavor. I loved it and was happy that I had the time to devote to playgroups, Mommy-and-me classes, and a host of other things that I had dreamed about all those years. But I wanted something just for me, so I began volunteering at the local meditation center. I was assigned to help out in the craft room of the Sunday school. Right up my alley, I thought: scissors, glue, glitter. It was all fun to me.

Those Sunday mornings were quiet during the hour and a half I was there. The woman in charge of crafts, Nora, was often busy shuttling between the classrooms, so I was left alone, usually with the supplies. I liked the quiet and the solitude sitting in my child-sized chair, tending to whatever project I was given.

One cold Sunday morning in January, I walked into the still chilly room and saw another woman sitting in my chair next to the portable space heater humming along. I stopped and felt cautious about this newcomer.

"Lily, meet Elizabeth Deschamps. She just moved here from Montreal." Nora motioned to the dark-haired woman sitting in my spot.

"Hello." She smiled. I detected a thick accent. Her eyes were kind, her dark bangs marched straight across her forehead. For some reason she reminded me of a character from my favorite childhood books, *Madeline*. I often read aloud to Colin the adventures of Madeline and her friends as they studied at their Parisian boarding school under the tutelage of Miss Clavel, their gentle teacher.

My mind went straight to the book:

In an old house in Paris
That was covered in vines
Lived twelve little girls
In two straight lines.

"Hi," I said, still standing in the doorway. Something about her made me pause and I felt an odd sensation of trying to take in this new person. I brought my hand to my chest. The area around my heart was heating up. It was peculiar. I had never felt anything like this.

I joined Elizabeth at the table, two thirty-something woman sitting knee to knee, in child-sized chairs at a table laden with magazines, construction paper, scissors and glue.

"We are supposed to cut these pictures out and glue them onto the paper." Whenever she said *the*, it sounded like *zee*. Whenever she said *pictures*, it sounded like *peektures*. She seemed shy and tentative with the language. Her thick French accent was beautiful, but my ears strained to make out each word.

It was like sitting across from Madeline, I thought. Nora must be Miss Clavel! Oh, how many times Miss Clavel attempted to keep Madeline and her friends out of trouble. I didn't think Elizabeth and I could get into much trouble here in the craft room, though.

Despite the language issues, we enjoyed our time at the tiny table and exchanged phone numbers. We had much in common, actually. Her only child, Simon, was four years old. Colin was now three. She had attended Catholic school as a child as had I, and we both took up meditation around the same point in our lives. She loved crafting as much as I did. Her husband's job had brought them across the country, just as we had done several years ago. But beyond the outward similarities, there was a comfort level that went beyond that. Maybe that had caused the warmth I felt in my chest when I first met her. The sensation felt like recognition of some kind. Odd for me, but I chose not to analyze it.

Our friendship grew quickly outside of the little craft room. I loved showing her the sights of southern California and she enjoyed all that our coastal area offered. She was making great strides in learning the language, but often our conversations were halting. Yet the language impediment might have deepened our friendship, I suspected. We often relied more on non-verbal exchanges, as they proved more reliable than her still-emerging English.

Keisha and I had spent years finessing our non-verbal exchanges, and Elizabeth and I now practiced similar skills. Our time spent together was different in many ways, despite our similarities. We had known one another only a few months but our bond seemed comfortable, deep and familial. We talked about it on several occasions and what might be at the root of this unexpected, but highly treasured friendship. I suspected that Elizabeth might have fallen into the category of soulmate, that phrase that James and I had discussed years before in the Afghan restaurant.

Being with a soulmate often felt like being shrouded in a cocoon—warm, nurturing and intimate. The rest of the world seemed to fade as you connected with your partner and traded laughter, tears, quiet confidences and even mundane things.

It had been a while since a soulmate had showed up!

Several months after our initial meeting, she called me.

"I have a surprise," she announced in her thick accent. She seemed giddy.

"We have been looking for a new home since our, what's the word ... landlord ... told us he's selling the house." She paused and I could feel her smile.

"We have rented the house down the street from you!"

"Really?" I screamed. "Great news! What fun we'll have." I missed having family near to me, especially now that I had a child. It felt like I was now going to have relatives living just a few doors away. Or maybe it would be just like the old house covered in vines where Madeline and her friends lived out their adventures.

Within two weeks, Colin, Keisha and I were in the Deschamps's new living room, five houses away from our own, helping to sift and sort through the moving boxes. Elizabeth's son Simon was kind and extremely intelligent; he seemed much older than his four years.

"Come on, Colin," he motioned to my son. His accent mimicked his mother's. "Let's play."

Colin seemed hesitant. He was often standoffish in new situations, and I was hoping he'd feel the immediate comfort level I had felt with Elizabeth. No such luck.

When a soulmate enters your life, you hope that the rest of your tribe accepts them and brings them into the fold. I was hoping that Colin would feel about Elizabeth and Simon as I did.

Simon patiently offered Colin toy after toy, but Colin continued to hang back while I started to feel a bit of anxiety that things were not going as smoothly as I wanted. Seeing Colin's hesitation, Elizabeth walked over to a large trunk and opened the lid.

"Why don't you boys see what's in the dress-up chest?"

I did not have anything like this at our house, and I thought Colin would surely not be interested.

Simon ran to the chest excitedly while Colin slowly walked towards the container filled with outfits, hats, and silly items. He leaned tentatively over to inspect the contents while Simon pulled items out onto the floor. I was becoming annoyed with Colin now, but then I saw his face change.

He reached in and pulled out some kind of hat, or cap, really. It was a tight yellow cap with a festoon of yellow feathers that sprouted alarmingly out of the top, resembling some kind of mutant chicken feathers. His face lit up as if he had hit a golden treasure. Elizabeth quickly stepped beside him and sorted through the items till she found a yellow caftan.

"Here!" she announced and handed it to Colin. "These will match well."

Colin inspected it and smiled. I could tell he was impressed with her stylist skills.

Attuned to their shared mission, they both rooted around some more and found two yellow rubber dishwashing gloves, along with a pair of over-sized sunglasses in a shocking neon green color. Elizabeth acted as his assistant as he donned the caftan, which puddled around his ankles and helped him place the chicken plume over his scalp, tucking his blonde hair beneath the cap. Next, the rubber gloves. They were huge and the ends swam around his elbows. Finally the piece d' resistance—the neon glasses. His tiny nose offered barely enough room for them to sit.

Colin literally beamed with pride over this outrageous, comical get-up. I had never seen him so pleased with himself.

Elizabeth clapped her hands together: "Magnifique!"

Simon looked on and smiled. Keisha barked an approval from the couch where she had been watching the show.

"You look like the Funky Chicken, Colin!" I laughed—a bit afraid I might have offended him.

He tilted his head and feathers flopped to the side. "The Thunky Chicken?" he tried to repeat.

"No, the Funky Chicken," I corrected, trying not to laugh more than I already was.

"Oh, I like Thunky Chicken better," Elizabeth offered.

Colin's smile spread across his face. He and Elizabeth shared a knowing look.

He had found a kindred spirit who understood good costuming and proper branding. Keisha's penchant for all things theatrical was well known and I was now suspecting she may have been secretly instructing Colin in the art as well. He lifted his chin in the slightest way so as to showcase the chicken plume at the proper angle. One gloved hand rested proudly on his hip while the other patted the headdress.

Elizabeth, Simon, and I all laughed and clapped our hands. While the Thunky Chicken was eating up the applause, Colin had taken the audience into his heart.

Chapter 37

"It takes a smart brunette to play a dumb blonde."
— Marilyn Monroe

While Colin had finally accepted Elizabeth as someone special, it seemed like Elizabeth was not necessarily appreciative of another soulmate of mine—Keisha. Often when we were gathered at our house, Keisha was, as usual, joyfully in the mix. Most people enjoyed engaging Keisha, her charms mostly irresistible. But I noticed Elizabeth watched Keisha from a distance.

Finally one day she offered, "I'm a cat lover. I've never been much of a dog person."

My heart sank. Who could NOT love a dog, I thought. And especially this one!

Keisha seemed unfazed by the lack of appreciation.

"She's very cat-like, though," Elizabeth added.

Yes, Keisha did have cat-like qualities, though I would never want to reveal that opinion to her. Keisha considered cats in the same category as squirrels. "She doesn't really seem like a dog," Elizabeth continued, appearing perplexed as her eyes looked at the snoozing dog.

Knowing that my new friend was blind to the charms of my dog, it was with reluctance that I asked Elizabeth to take care of her for a week. James had business in New Orleans during the height of the Mardi Gras festivities, and Colin, my parents, and I were traveling with him. Julia was not available to offer Keisha a place to hang out, so I thought Elizabeth's close proximity might be a good solution.

"Are you sure? I've never taken care of a dog before." I could tell she was uncomfortable with the request.

"It's easy," I offered. "Feed her twice a day and take her for walks afterward." Then I cautiously added, "And give her some affection, too. I don't want her to be lonely."

I could see Elizabeth's inner conflict: wanting to offer assistance but clearly this fell beyond her comfort zone. Once she accepted, though, she threw herself into the task with vigor.

"Look," she said breathlessly one afternoon as she stood at my front door. She was holding a spiral notebook with her long, graceful hands. "I can keep a captain's log of my caretaking of Keisha!" She seemed immensely pleased with herself and was having fun with the challenge of caring for her new charge. Keisha appeared nonplussed by the events. I suspected she was actually looking forward to having the house to herself for a week. She often sought out quiet spots lately, away from the household noise.

New Orleans was a rollicking celebration with Colin draped in colorful beads and sporting a king's crown as we toured the French Quarter in a horse-drawn carriage. Between beignets and Hurricanes, I checked in on Operation Keisha. Yes, the Captain's Log was being meticulously maintained. I could read the details when I returned.

"Star Date: 47457.1. The mission is proceeding well; all systems are functioning within acceptable parameters."

I did read through the log once we were home. It was fastidiously maintained and spoke to the level of care that Elizabeth afforded her ward. Although she was technically the captain, I sensed the real leader had been Keisha. She was quite adept at getting her needs met in any situation.

I also sensed that something deeper had transpired during those days of caretaking. Their relationship had been changed to an unspoken connection of trust and understanding. I never asked her about it. It seemed too intimate.

Relationships were unique and complex. What transpired between two parties was often best left between them alone.

Colin, Keisha, and I now made frequent trips to Austin to visit my parents, now proud grandparents. James stayed behind for work. Keisha and Colin occupied the backseat together and made great traveling partners.

My dog loved to visit her second home in Texas and the squirrels there managed to give her a run for her money during those times. As we walked the streets of Rollinghills, we often waved a greeting as the patrolling police car rolled by.

Nice to see old friends, Keisha seemed to say.

I had often thought back to Maggie's reference to the illicit coupling of the black Chow and the husky next door. She had foretold that Keisha would reach 60-70 pounds, yet Keisha had maintained a steady weight of about 35 pounds most of her life. She never reached the height of either a chow or a husky, nor their temperament. When we hosted play groups at our house, I noticed Keisha's instinctual herding behavior as she circled the children and tried to move them into a tighter pack.

I wondered what genes really did spiral along her DNA. It didn't matter, I guess. She had turned out to be quite different in so many ways from original expectations. But I found that to be true in so much of life.

James was traveling more and more for business now, and Keisha most often stayed behind while Colin and I tagged along. Julia, Keisha's longtime roommate, welcomed her on those occasions with open arms, and Keisha pranced off for her stay with her old friend, never failing to bring a bit of excitement to Julia's household which now included a husband and daughter.

"Look, look!" her toddler would say, pointing a chubby finger at the window overlooking the front lawn.

There, peering inside with an ear to ear grin would be Keisha, who had managed to escape the confines of the fenced backyard.

Catch me if you can, the dark eyes cajoled. And off Julia ran to play Keisha's game of cat and mouse.

But Julia found an opportunity to harness Keisha's love of the dramatic in a less dangerous way that involved my old roommate's love of morning-radio and an avid fan of a local show hosting two raucous and irreverent DJs. One morning while Keisha was vacationing at Julia's house, the DJs sent out a call for any dogs who could bark on-command to participate in a production of a Sam-Spade-type radio play.

Knowing Keisha's reflexive barking response to a knocking at the door, Julia leapt to the phone and twenty minutes later Keisha was poised to make her radio debut as Trixie, the gum chewing, red-lipstick-wearing, street-smart gal who frequented the local pool halls and speak-easies. Standing next to Julia and the kitchen phone, she waited eagerly to deliver her lines for FM 101's premier of *The Red Fire Hydrant Caper*.

At 10 o'clock that morning, the pipe organs heralded the start of the canine production and soon the drama began to unfold as the swarthy detective, Dan Diamond, began to unravel the mystery of the crime committed just feet from the metal hydrant. Diamond's paws stepped through the door of the gin-joint across the street to interview any witnesses to the crime. As he stealthily asked questions of the seductive Trixie, she answered the gumshoe with sassy but flirtatious barks, always preceded by Julia's knocking on the kitchen cabinet. Her performance was nuanced but riveting.

"I know dames like you, Trixie," Diamond said.

Dan's bark was low and even.

"You play coy, but you know more than you're saying."

Trixie was poised to answer his accusation.

KNOCK, KNOCK.

Trixie barked again. Woo woo woo.

"I'm just a small town gal, Dan. I don't know much other than your pokin' around in some dangerous areas." You could practically hear the gum smacking in her delivery.

A pause in the action occurred, however, as one of the DJ's voices traveled through the radio waves: "Do you guys notice that there is always some sort of mysterious knocking right before Trixie speaks?"

Julia blanched a bit. Keisha's method acting was being exposed. Despite the well-timed, background knocking, the drama played out until the final and shocking revelation of the perpetrator. The whole production had been recorded and the talented cast had been awarded a taste of notoriety and a cassette tape of the broadcast.

As we walked through the door that night to pick Keisha up from her stay, the starlet was lounging on the couch with Julia's daughter, playing with a stuffed animal. Julia handed us the recording and we all chuckled at Keisha's premiere performance. She had entertained us all for years, and now her talents had sashayed onto the air waves.

Keisha scratched her ear and delicately sniffed the end of her paw. A star was born.

The next week the starlet headed to the vet's for an annual check-up—surely another opportunity to let the drama-queen exercise her talents. True to form, Keisha offered the theatrics for which she was well known and the red dot on her file seemed to glow extra brightly that day. Dr. Nash strained to hold her still, while his stethoscope moved along her chest. He stopped and his brows furrowed. My heart began beating quickly, without a stethoscope to broadcast the pounding. He stepped back and grabbed the X-rays that had been taken of Keisha's chest months before, showing the lump of muscle nestled inside the cage of rib bone. We both stared at the black and gray images. My eyes moved to watch Dr. Nash's face.

"I'm hearing a bit more of a pronounced echo of the heart murmur," he finally said.

He turned back to Keisha, still glaring at him with dark eyes, and placed the stethoscope on her chest again.

"Her lungs are clear though. I think it's just the normal progression as the dog ages. Nothing to worry about. We'll just monitor things. I don't see any need for alarm."

Well, I do, I thought. But I tended to keep my dark thoughts to myself.

The appointment was wrapped up and Keisha pulled me out of the office, my mood significantly darker than when we entered. My relieved dog eagerly jumped in the car and we headed back to the house. She was, once again, hanging precariously out of the car window, immersed in roadway bliss as the car sped home. But I wanted to stop time. I wanted everything to freeze so that nothing moved forward. *This was fine, thank you.*

But I couldn't stop time. It marched on. I could watch Colin and his body respond to time. He grew and changed and expanded to his new self. But at some point we all reach some sort of crest and time begins a different kind of progression. The shift was subtle at first and then tended to gain speed. You were on the back curve of the race. And time moved forward whether you like it or not.

I looked over again at the Doggie Lama, dangling from the car window, seemingly oblivious to anything but the blast of the wind. I pictured her little heart inside, only I knew its size was not normal. It would not beat forever. One day it would stop and I would have to go on. Without her.

I had always been a melancholy person, but motherhood had heightened this trait to a new level. Watching Colin grow had allowed me to see clearly how fast time did leave its mark.

As we pulled into the driveway, I turned off the car and sat for a moment with Keisha and my dark thoughts beside me. I petted her silky fur and she kissed my hand. I shivered at the thought of not having her beside me. My own heart felt heavy and filled with fear.

Yet sitting there in the quiet of the car, beside my friend, the gloomy thoughts reluctantly stepped aside to allow another awareness to fill the space:

there were so many, many things I had learned from this crazy dog.

I fingered the end of her leash, tucked under her belly. I had held the reins of her leash all these years but who was guiding whom? She was my teacher in so many ways. She instructed not from a list of platitudes or a manual, but from her very essence and her approach to life:

The earthly plane was filled with sensory desires and it was not a bad thing to be enticed—a bag of powdery donuts, a garbage pail filled with aromatic temptations. A Mardi Gras celebration of old shag carpet and padding—*delight in those things of this world, the consequences can be dealt with when they arise.*

Don't be afraid to make friends with a wide array of people. You can cavort with fighter pilots as you watch a raucous football game. Enjoy Mexican food with a handsome guy in a convertible or spend a quiet evening reading a book beside a dear friend. Equally, don't be afraid to make it known who you prefer to live without: pesky squirrels, taunting neighbor dogs, or a villainous-looking Santa at the pet store. And when confronted with even more dangerous opponents, embrace the red dot! Stand your ground and fight, or muster all resources for a quick and life-saving escape. 23 Skidoo!

Push your boundaries a bit. Test the forces that confine you and expand your adventure beyond what you, or others, think you can. You may be surprised where it leads you.

Keisha knew nothing about money or time, both finite resources. I wrestled with both endlessly, it seemed. *Sometimes,* she urged, *you gotta let go and stop counting everything.*

But as I looked at her dark, glistening eyes she reminded me that all of that is of the earthly variety.

The space beyond physical form was just as real and offered its own delight. She seemed to instruct me in the art of feeling beyond the physical, to the energy that informs our world and beyond. And even our individual connection to it. I watched her as she stretched her body so often, feeling into the movement and responding to the flow of energy, and encouraging those stuck places to open and get filled up.

Her joy as she pushed out through the car window and absorbed the wind, the smells, the entirety of our journey down the road. The universe was a wondrous place!

Her perceptions of my energy field during meditation, as I began exploring the space beyond my physical body. And my search to understand my place and connection to a larger existence.

She knew love—receiving it and giving it. It was real, tangible. But unlike us humans, she wasn't wary of it nor did she grasp for it. It just WAS. Like the air we breathed. Or the sunlight we absorbed. She didn't need to earn it nor did the love she gave depend on worthiness.

The offer of a powdered donut might make the transaction sweeter, though.

Love was not a commodity or a bargaining chip. It was there—real and for the taking.

We hadn't traveled the globe to exotic locales. We hadn't navigated dangerous and exciting adventures. We didn't travel to the Himalayas to sit at the feet of a wise guru, seeking enlightenment. We sat on the floor of the spare bedroom beside one another, breathing in and out. The vast universe was right there behind closed eyes, an open mind, and a willing heart.

We had joined forces daily to journey through love and connection. Through illness and stolen snacks. Through depleted bank accounts and tiny vermin that munched away at fur. Through nightly snuggles and life-saving surgeries. Through sadistic squirrels and jobs that were less than fulfilling. Through discovering soulmates along our path and savoring every moment with them.

No one would ever make a movie out of our journey; these were just the things of everyday life, the substance of the physical earth. But our connection had been an epic tale, in my opinion.

Or maybe just an epic *tail*, as Keisha may have thought.

She was instructing me, I suspected, in this subtle play of a paradox—to be a spiritual, energetic being while at the same time living a physical, earthly experience. The two concepts seemed to be at odds most of the time, and yet where the two notions bumped up against each other was a place of magic.

We were separate, each encased in our own body-homes, but we were more than that. We were all part of this mystical, magnificent universe, and it flowed around us and through us. We were all stardust, dancing through the cosmos. She didn't chant mantras, read holy texts, do special breathing techniques or recite sacred prayers—she lived with ease. She felt joy and she gave joy.

My thoughts were flooded with the lessons delivered to me through the years by this little dog as we lived beside one another exploring the world, even at times apart, and I felt a sense of awe or sacredness in the relationship with this funny, complex, and mystical being. I had invited her into my life as my protector, to keep me safe from harm. And in some ways she had done quite the opposite. She had opened up the space around my wounded and fearful heart. She had laid it bare and allowed me to let in so many, many wonderful things that I may not have otherwise allowed in.

Maybe that sound that woke me so many nights ago at 2:34 a.m. had been Keisha, poking at the lock on my heart.

I grabbed her face and buried my own in her fur. The smell was familiar and comforting. I breathed it in. I never wanted to lose her. Ever. But I knew the laws of the physical world where nothing lasted. I breathed her in one more time to try and anchor it into my brain and store it for the unknown future. The car was quiet. I grabbed her leash and we headed for the house.

Life was waiting.

Chapter 38

*"People don't resist change.
They resist being changed."*
— Peter M. Senge

I was born into a family that seemed to have an odd obsession with death. Funerals were something to be planned with great forethought and precision. Music, attire, lighting at the viewing—all elements that would set the tone. Beyond the theater of the production, the mystery of death and what lies beyond this life were at the heart of the matter. Our loved ones journeyed into the unknown while the rest of us were left here to continue on our path, knowing someday we would learn, too, if and what may wait for us on the other side.

It was when my maternal grandmother had passed that I had my first deep experience of saying goodbye to someone I loved immensely and releasing them to this great unknown. I was twenty five years old and had recently said my goodbyes to *him* only months before.

I stood in the cemetery as the priest spoke the ritual words over my grandmother's casket sitting temporarily next to the unearthed hole in the ground. I stood, locking my knees, as the wind teased a stray hair across my face. It seemed to invite the tears that wanted to flow. I saw my cousin reach for his wife and hold onto her; it was comforting to watch. My tears wanted to flow in a violent storm, along with an audible sob and I, too, wanted to lean my weight into a loved one so that they might hold me up, for just a bit, while I said goodbye to this person who meant the world to me.

The previous night at the viewing I saw her hands crossed over her chest where her heart no longer beat, with a gleaming rosary intertwined between her fingers. These same hands had rested across hospital sheets only a month ago. They seemed different as the nurses had tucked her wedding ring in the bedside stand. I held them, as we talked and laughed and never really addressed what we knew was coming.

Those hands had taught me to cook, to bake, to crochet and to do needlepoint. They had grabbed my own hands in the dark, while she and I quietly waited for sleep in her old brass bed.

But now those hands were in the metal box, and I would never touch them again.

The tears came in a torrent and I wanted, needed, someone to hold onto. I wanted *him* to be standing next to me and comfort me the way that only *his* presence could. But he was not there. Our 'goodbye' had already been said.

I wiped the tears, held my breath and tightened my knees.

A few months later, I reached for my hairbrush on a typical morning ritual and stopped. I looked at the brush that I used every day and saw it as if for the first time. My grandmother had given it to me almost twenty years ago. My fine hair was notorious for working itself into unmanageable knots, and she had gifted me with an expensive boars-head brush to help me tame my unruly strands. After twenty years of service, it was missing a fair amount of bristles and the handle was stained and chipped in a few places but it still did the job, smoothing my hair into some semblance of order.

The task my grandmother had given it all those years ago.

As I looked at it then, it occurred to me that I would not see her ever again, as if I were hearing the news for the first time. It seemed so final, holding her brush as I had done a million times but coming to an abrupt, breathtaking realization that she was completely, irrevocably gone from my life.

But quickly on the heels of that gut-wrenching awareness came another odd sensation—it felt as if she were right next to me. But not in the normal physical, skin-to-skin way. It was pervasive, and my mind tried to process a feeling I had not ever remembered having previously. Her essence seemed to penetrate the air around me, but even beyond that. It was her, but it was something greater than her.

Later I would come across a book that described some Native American beliefs about death and the departed soul's immersion into the Great Spirit. As I read the words, an image of a colored liquid being poured into a larger vessel of water emerged in my thoughts. The inkiness flowed into the water and dispersed itself in its new home, joining and becoming part of the greater whole. That was the closest that I had come to describing that moment of feeling my grandmother.

While she resided here on earth, in her physical body, I would need to travel to her little house on Elm Street, or dial the phone to reach her at the other end, or walk into the other room to sit beside her. But now I need only to turn my focus on the Great Spirit that infuses everything. She surrounded me, she flowed through me.

It was an experience I kept to myself. My Catholic upbringing instructed a depiction of the after-life that I had accepted comfortably. This visceral sensation was different and I struggled to comprehend it and reconcile it with my previous beliefs. I didn't quite understand it and I certainly didn't want to share it. It was personal and intimate. And I didn't want it to be misunderstood.

The summer of Colin's fourth year, I felt immensely misunderstood.

It had started out to be a stressful one. James had been traveling non-stop and it was taking its toll. I was experiencing a series of health problems: blinding headaches, nausea and a general sense of dis-ease. Keisha had begun to act in strange ways lately; seemingly not hearing me when I called her or wandering off down the street. One afternoon I found her standing in the pond in the backyard, just staring into space.

She was different and I could feel it. Changes in her flowed to me and others noticed that I was behaving differently. When I tried to explain what I was feeling, what I feared might be happening, I was often met with a quizzical look. Or perhaps some compassion but it turned quickly to offers to brush it off, to not worry.

I'm not sure anyone else ever really understood the connection between Keisha and me. I could feel the judgment of some: "It's just a dog." Others, who understood our bond, didn't seem to want to spend much time entertaining the emotions that come from the ending of that connection. So I moved through my days feeling the changes that were transpiring in my friend despite the vet's pronouncement that he could not detect anything serious going on. I shoved down the waves of fear and moved along with life. I often thought back to that moment of holding my grandmother's brush and the odd and comforting awareness that came, but it did little to assuage my resistance to what I felt was coming.

Chapter 39

"Until one has loved an animal, part of their soul remains unawakened."
— Anatole France

It was a summer laden with stress. It was also the summer of Keisha's 14th birthday. I thought back to Jonathan's foretelling of Heartache City. I felt heavy with dread.

James's presence often calmed me down and offered an anchor to the unmooring of my thoughts, but he was spending inordinate amounts of time in Detroit and I was shouldering a lot alone. We had planned a trip for Colin, Keisha, and me to travel in early August for a two-week stay in Austin, to coincide with a very long trip of James's. I was looking forward to the respite.

The heavy feeling of that summer increased with the news that Elizabeth and her family would return to Montreal for her husband's job. I was heartsick; I had come to rely on her presence for support and much-needed laughter and lightness. Their move, scheduled for August 8, four days after Keisha's 14th birthday, left me with a feeling of dread and loneliness.

The dates loomed on my calendar.

As my headaches relentlessly continued, I began to experience waves of panic—free-floating anxiety that grabbed me out of nowhere. They seized my ribs like a vise and squeezed, making it hard to breathe. As I managed our schedule of playdates and outings for Colin, I also began a series of vet visits to determine what was going on with Keisha. Her bloodwork revealed nothing of great concern, her heart condition had not progressed, and she showed no sign of deafness. The vet suspected several things, one being a case of doggie Alzheimer's. He wrote a prescription for a very expensive drug and said to check back with him in a few weeks.

She seemed fine most of the time, yet the moments of deafness, of confusion and now constant peeing and pooping on the living-room carpet were all signs that something was amiss. We began the prescribed drug and hoped for the best.

After dropping James off at the airport one Sunday afternoon for another week-long trip, we turned into a drive-thru to pick up some dinner, as I was too tired to cook anything. Colin was sleeping in the backseat with Keisha in her normal spot beside me. I steered the car beside the order station and glanced over at Keisha. She had slumped in the seat and her body had stiffened in an alarming way. Urine poured down the leather seat, and I screamed and stared in horror. It lasted only a moment and her body softened.

"May I take your order?" The speaker droned from the lighted outdoor menu on my left.

I couldn't speak. I turned to the scene on my right. I stroked her fur and felt her body relax further. Her breathing returned to normal.

"Hello? May I take your order?"

I sat frozen. I let out my breath.

Keisha sat up and blinked.

"I um ... I'd like to order two burgers, please." This was surreal.

Colin had awoken.

"What's wrong, Mommy?" His eyes were wide with fear.

"Keisha is sick," I said, trying to keep the panic from my voice. As my body thawed, I could feel that familiar wave of anxiety begin to take hold.

Just get the food and get home. Somehow getting home was my only course of action.

Through the fog, I completed the transaction, drove the short distance home and by the time we pulled into the driveway Keisha was back to normal. She trotted out of the car and up to the door as if nothing had happened. We all walked inside, Colin sat at the table with his food, and Keisha followed me to the phone.

I collapsed on the floor and dialed James.

"I can't do this," I breathed. "I can't do this alone."

"What's going on?" he said. He sounded panicked, too.

I began to cry and I couldn't stop. Keisha was turning fourteen. Heartache City. It was happening. And I wasn't strong enough to do this. James was 1,500 miles away. I was alone. I had to take care of

Colin. And I had to face whatever was happening to Keisha.

"I can't do this by myself," I cried.

I somehow managed to tell him what had happened. I watched Keisha as I recounted the events, but she stared back at me intently seemingly normal now.

"Call the vet and take her in." James's calmness always centered me. I hung up and called the vet whose recording gave the number for the emergency vet office. It was Sunday. Back in the car, we navigated to the address I was given. My head started to pound. Only Colin's presence kept me from outwardly displaying the chaos I felt inside.

Three hours later we emerged into the dark parking lot with an unclear diagnosis. Yes, it was a seizure, but the cause was unclear. Keisha jogged to the car with no evidence of any medical issue. I felt exhausted and we headed home to the empty house.

The living room carpet was now stained with urine and feces as Keisha continued to soil the floor day after day. My attempts to clean the odorous blotches left the rug patch worked with puddles of crispy, bleached fibers. It was a health hazard now and the smell was pungent. Although she had slept with me her entire life, now we were discussing the need to keep her in a tiled area through the night.

One night of her recriminations proved the folly of that approach.

Yet most often she chose to sleep outside the bedroom door, in the hallway, eschewing her normal position in the crook of my legs. The medication seemed to do little to shift the dementia symptoms and the vet still had no indication as to the source of the seizures. The stains in the carpet grew in number and the frequency of the seizures increased. But the most painful part for me was the more frequent disconnection from her surroundings. She felt further and further away from me. She rarely snuggled with me.

She was getting me ready to be on my own, I decided.

The date on the calendar loomed ahead: August 2, Keisha's 14th birthday. I needed to get that damn number out of my head. I cursed Jonathan every time I thought of it. Early in July we decided that something must be done about the carpeting so we gathered at the kitchen table and ran the numbers of alternative flooring.

The carpeting ran continuously throughout the downstairs except for the kitchen. If we replaced the living room flooring we needed to run whatever we chose throughout the rest of the downstairs and aesthetically it would look better to continue into the kitchen. But hardwood had been ruled out and it made no sense to replace the old flooring with a new layer of carpet she would soil. The numbers were tallied and a clear winner emerged: tile.

Practical. Easy-to-clean. And my least favorite.

Cold. Hard. Austere.

Tile it was.

"Okay, Keisha," I told her one afternoon. "We are going with tile because of how much I love you. I'm expecting you to stick around for a while."

Her dark lashes blinked. It was unclear how she received the message—one of both fear and hope.

Construction on the floor began in mid-July and Colin, Keisha, and I moved upstairs for a week. James was out of town again and I was left tending to the house, Keisha's fluctuating health, and my own physical symptoms. I always had loved the summer months; they seemed so carefree. But now we were relegated to the upstairs as the tile saw buzzed away.

Now, I just wanted the summer to end. I wanted everything to shift.

The flooring was completed and I saw it as a solid commitment to Keisha's health and her choosing to stay with us a while. I stared at the six-thousand dollar investment and decided I disliked it as much as I predicted: cold, rigid and lending a cavernous feeling to the downstairs. The things we do for love!

Our scheduled trip to Texas was fast approaching and I desperately needed the break. But it was becoming clear that Keisha would probably not be able to travel the long distance through the desert. Her seizures were now becoming more frequent, and her sensory processing was declining quickly. The vet was still puzzled as to what was going on; he had not uncovered what was at the root of the symptoms.

I felt trapped by the circumstances and my anxiety was now a constant hum. I could not face two weeks here, alone without James, dealing with what now seemed to be the imminent exit of my beloved Keisha. I wanted to run away, and the safest place seemed to be to Austin, to my childhood home, where I could be petted and cared for by my mom and dad. Perhaps that feeling of heavy responsibility I had felt so acutely that night in the hospital room four years earlier had not been fully healed. I had felt overwhelmed by the events around Colin's birth. I was a mother, and I fully accepted all that comes with that. But a part of me wanted to be someone's child again. I didn't want the responsibility. Certainly not of this.

So we began to strategize about where Keisha might stay while we were in Texas. She seemed so disconnected to me anyway that I felt she might not even miss me. And I entertained the possibility that perhaps she and I needed to be apart so that she could leave on her own.

My friend Corinne, who was at our house often with her children, kindly stepped forward and said she would care for Keisha while we were gone. She knew the responsibility of that task and yet she offered her help; she could see how much pain I was in.

We had just celebrated Keisha's birthday a few days earlier with our usual cake and song. I tried to smile through the melody and seem upbeat, as I felt the tile floor beneath my feet. It was tangible evidence that we were investing in her future. But I couldn't get that momentous birthday out of my head.

The day before our trip we headed to Corinne's for a trial run at her house for Keisha's stay. I needed assurance that Keisha would be comfortable there and feel safe. I had high hopes that this option would work.

Colin, Keisha and I walked through the gate of Corinne's backyard and all eyes turned to meet us and welcome Keisha. She seemed good that morning and things felt strong. Optimism flowed through me, making me feel strong, too. Colin ran to meet his friends, and Corinne and I began to discuss Keisha's care. She assured me that she would be well-tended and not to worry. The children ran back over to Keisha, petting her and talking to her, but she seemed overwhelmed by the attention and I saw her body stiffen.

My heart sank. I knew then we had pushed things too far.

I lifted her up and carried her to the front porch where it was quiet and I could hold her. I sat on the step and cradled her in my arms. Oddly, my anxiety had not joined us on the porch and it occurred to me that this may be the opportunity to say goodbye. I think she sensed that something was happening and she didn't seem able to cope with this environment.

I wanted to be strong for her—to hold a space for her to let go. She wouldn't do it, I thought, if I was falling apart. I sat there and cradled her. Just her and me—the founding members of the pack.

"I'm here," I whispered close to her ear, "just you and me. I know what's happening and that you've been preparing me. I'll be okay. You need to know that. So if you need to leave, you can. This is an okay time ... it's just you and me. Just like we started."

I continued to cradle her stiff body as the seizure came. And I waited for the awful thing that I did not think I could withstand. I waited, I held her and I poured out my love for her. There on the front porch. It was as if two friends were waiting in the airport terminal for the flight to be called. The PA system would announce the departure flight, my friend would stand and walk toward her journey and board the plane. And I would stay behind, waving farewell.

We sat for a while waiting for the announcement. I was oddly calm and we both sat, cocooned in our shared love for one another, waiting.

But she turned back.

I could feel her body fill back up. She softened and soon she had pulled away from me and stood by the door. Her tail wagged. She wanted to return to the backyard.

Chapter 40

> *"To say goodbye is to die a little."*
> — Raymond Chandler
> The Long Goodbye

That night I lay in bed unsure as to what to do. I didn't know where she could stay if we traveled. But I didn't think I could stay home, alone, and wait for what was surely coming.

Tomorrow was the dreaded day that Elizabeth and her family would be leaving. The boxes were packed waiting for the movers, and once they had been loaded into the van, the Deschamps family was boarding a flight to Canada.

I could hear James snoring beside me.

I remembered the line from the original *Father of the Bride*, when Spencer Tracy battled a sleepless night filled with worry and anxiety over the future. He leaned over and woke his wife, poured his fears to her side of the bed and leaned back, unburdened.

"Well, I got it off my chest," I could hear Tracy's voiceover. "Funny, the minute you get someone else worrying, you stop worrying yourself."

I shook James awake. And unburdened myself.

But Spencer's strategy was failing me.

Neither of us knew what to do. These years had at least shown me that when at a crossroads like this, when the path is unclear, prayer or silent communion with what's beyond us can bring miracles.

"Let's just pray," I said in the stillness. We had nothing to lose. I closed my eyes and we each leaned into the darkness, sending our requests for help into the ethers. The tears began to flow and I was overcome. I was completely at a loss. I listened to the dark stillness and before long I could hear James's snoring resume. So he had reached a level of peace, I guess.

I opened my eyes, still clouded with tears and blinked.

The room was dark and noiseless and yet at the foot of the bed I saw something strange. It was some kind of luminescence slowly swirling in the air, purple in color. Lavender, actually. It was about two feet wide and I couldn't see how far it reached below but it extended upwards about four feet from the edge of the bed. Whatever it was spiraled in a counter-clockwise motion and sparkling silver specks danced in the revolving light. It was beautiful.

I blinked again. Maybe the tears in my eyes were causing me to see this mirage. Its colors, its sparkles, its ethereal quality was soothing to the place of pain that engulfed me. I rubbed my eyes so I could clear my vision. It was still there. I had never seen anything like this; maybe I should wake James. Or call for help. Clearly I was having a break with reality.

Yet I didn't want to move. Or to stop looking at it.

After a moment, I closed my eyes and breathed. My body relaxed. My pain and anguish were easing. I breathed more.

I opened my eyes again and searched for the purple light but it was gone. I blinked and massaged my eyes again. The room was dark and there was no trace of the light. I lay motionless in the blackness of the room until a deep sleep finally fell over me.

The next morning, the day we were scheduled to begin our drive to Texas, nothing had been resolved about Keisha. Or so I thought.

James had gone into the office to settle a few things, and I awoke full of apprehension. Should I just cancel? Should I try and take her with us? The dilemma returned in full force to my body.

I looked around the sunlit room. It seemed in direct contrast to the darkness and heaviness I felt inside. I sat and cleared my eyes. And then I remembered my weird, other-worldly purple light from last night. Its beautiful, glistening, swirling luminescence.

I looked at the foot of the bed to see where it had been. Only sunlight now.

I walked to the foot of the bed and saw Keisha sleeping there. In the last few months, she had abandoned her normal sleeping position in the crook of my bent legs and often opted instead to sleep downstairs or outside my bedroom door. Our fourteen years of nightly snuggles were over. But this morning she was at the foot of the bed, curled snoot to tail.

She was positioned directly in the spot where the purple light had been shining, through my tears. Panic swept over me and I reached down, expecting to feel her cold, rigid body. But it was warm and soft and was filled with her Keisha-ness. She lifted her head and looked at me. Her eyes were clear and she seemed like her old self. I experienced only a moment of gratitude, as the awareness of the current situation was still not resolved.

I needed to shower and get dressed. Then I could think better. Keisha followed me into the bathroom and settled onto the floor. I watched her through the glass shower door and I saw her body stiffen in that way it had done so many times now. I ran from the shower and put my hand on her. Water streamed down from my hands and face and landed in her soft fur. Urine poured onto the tile floor from beneath her tail. The seizure lasted longer than it normally did, and it took her longer to soften and come back.

She lay on the floor, stiffening, while I quickly put my clothes on. She finally pulled herself onto her four legs and looked at me expectantly. We both stood facing one another while I battled for the next step. I asked her if she wanted to go downstairs. She blinked and began to follow me but stopped after a few steps as another seizure took hold.

For the next thirty minutes, I sat with her on the floor. It was then that I knew the beautiful purple light and the peace that I felt from it were an answer to our prayers. She was telling me in her own charming and beautiful way.

She would not be traveling with us to Texas. She had another journey to make.

I slowly got up and went to the phone. I called James and told him all that had transpired. He was home within 20 minutes. I continued to cradle Keisha on the floor as we waited for James. The odd dementia energy had seemed to clear and it felt pure and simple, almost reminiscent of when she was a puppy. James walked into the room, looking at both of us. He looked ghastly and I felt deep compassion for him.

"I called the vet. Do you want to go with us?" His voice was tight and strained.

My own voice didn't work. My throat was too tight. I was having trouble breathing. I shook my head. We were moving forward.

James lifted her up. Her head was limp and he cradled it against his shoulder.

I can't do this, I thought.

But some larger part of me knew that we had to. And Keisha knew it, too.

I stood up. James moved Keisha closer to me with his arms and said, "Do you want to say goodbye?"

At that moment I thought I might black out. The room closed in, my breath caught in my throat and my body stiffened. All I could muster was a step forward. I buried my face in her fur. No words came but my love poured out in waves. At that I stepped back, and ran to the bedroom.

As I curled on the bed in the fetal position I heard the front door close and the car start. I had no place to run away from this. It was happening. My best friend was leaving and the world would be empty without her. How could I go on?

The phone rang and I let the recorder answer. The announcement played and I heard the beep.

"Lily, its Elizabeth. The movers are here and I wanted to make sure we had time together today before we leave. Call me and let me know when you can come by."

I had forgotten about the other exit that was happening today. Too many goodbyes. Too many things being ripped from my grasp. I continued to lay there, curled in the middle of the bed, waiting. I looked at the clock: 10:15. Waves of pain and tightness flowed over me as I tried to feel what my world without Keisha would be. The aching came in a flood, a tsunami of tightness and constriction. It became unbearable, but at that moment something shifted. I was released from the confines of my tight and pained body. The constraints of the pain dissolved and the ache floated away. My body seemed to evaporate. My breath stopped and I felt something akin to bliss, how Keisha must surely have felt was she was driving with her head out the window.

In that space, I knew this was beyond me.

It was as surreal as the purple light from last night.

I knew, in that space within my heart, that this was what Keisha was now feeling.

I looked at the clock: 10:23 a.m. I wanted to mark the time of this moment, for some reason.

The peace flowed over me and I had a glimpse of what the yogis have described as our true nature, beyond the constraints of the physical body. And I reveled in it with Keisha. It WAS bliss.

Unmeasured time passed and finally I heard the front door open. I listened as James's footsteps worked their way toward me. He looked deflated, drawn, and defeated. My eyes questioned and he shook his head. I stood up and walked to him. We stood there, next to where the purple light had been, and hugged. We stood for a very long time, in a full embrace, in a world where Keisha no longer lived.

The rest of the morning was spent collecting ourselves and setting things in order now that decisions had been made. We would leave on our trip the next morning. We explained to Colin what had happened. He had witnessed the things Keisha's body had experienced and, like most children, seemed to accept what had happened with an equanimity that adults often find difficult.

"I think she's happy, Mommy," he said, looking into my eyes. There was wisdom in those sweet blue eyes, and I took it into my wounded spirit.

We were feeling more stable now, and James had gone to pick up something for us to eat, so I called my parents to let them know what had happened and to update them on our travels. I delivered the news to my mother who began to try and say something reassuring, as she always did. But the words stopped abruptly. Her throat constricted, just as mine had earlier. I could hear and feel the pain catch in her throat. We both sat on the line in silence. Tears streamed down my face and then my pain found its voice. It poured out in rivulets of agony as my mom sat on the other end, crying with me. The pain that had stopped so abruptly on the bed at 10:23 now came roaring back.

After a while, we gathered ourselves and moved onto the logistics of our upcoming visit. I ended the call and began to feel the first inklings of the terrible headaches I had been experiencing. I let Colin know that I was going to bed and to wait for Daddy and the food. I crawled into the spot where I had been at 10:23, and I could feel the muscles in my head tighten like a vise and my stomach begin to churn. Within twenty minutes, the migraine was incapacitating.

James came upstairs to lower the shades and make the room as quiet and dark as possible.

"Sweetie," he whispered. "Elizabeth has called twice to see if you can come say goodbye. They are leaving in an hour."

I moved my head from side to side. It hurt too much to talk. But the movement of my head poked the lion that was my headache and it roared back. I rolled over on my side, turning my back to James, and placed my arms over my head. He understood and rubbed his hand along my back gently.

One departure done. One under way.

He tip-toed out of the room, closed the door and left me in the quiet tomb of my pain.

I slept on and off amidst the physical pain. Drifting off, I could escape it but then I'd awaken and feel it and remember what had happened. I did not like this world without her.

I awoke at twilight. I could hear the television downstairs and the voices of Colin and James. The new tile floor made the sounds echo from the first floor. It was hollow and felt especially empty tonight. The tile floor—the symbol of Keisha staying with us a bit longer. I pictured the floor and then I saw Keisha's water and food bowl sitting in the corner. They would not be needed now. Someone needed to pick them up and put them away. But I couldn't move right now; the pain was too intense. My head throbbed.

Elizabeth was gone by now. On a plane, headed toward her new home. My head pounded, my stomach moved in waves of nausea but my chest felt heavy and cold.

Migraines often bring a sensitivity to sound, sight and smell. Any movement or noise could feel like a bomb exploding in the body. As I lay on the bed, my senses heightened, I noticed something in the room that seemed to stir the air a bit. It was familiar and I felt the same thing I had so many times when I had lain on the bed engulfed in a migraine. I was aware of Keisha, at the side of the bed, bringing her snoot to the edge, sniffing and checking on me. It was crisp and clear. My eyes flew open and I looked at the edge of the bed, sure that I would see her. The space was empty.

I closed my eyes again. But I could feel it — sniffing and inquiring.

Then I became aware of something else. A tug in the center of my chest. It didn't hurt but there was a pulling. I kept my eyes closed and tried to trace the source of the tugging. The pressure ran down a kind of cord, over and around to the side of the bed where I had imagined the sniffing dog. I could see in my mind's eye the cord travel to the center of the little dog that stood beside the bed, checking on me.

She was here! I could feel it. I traced it from my own body to her. I felt, in every cell of my body, that whatever Keisha was still existed. Her body had left, I had felt that, too. But now I knew in some way beyond logic and sight that the being that I had connected with still resided here with me. The pain of the migraine had made me excruciatingly sensitive to the physical world, but it offered me a door to feel that which resides beyond the physical.

I reveled in feeling her presence. It was familiar and happy. And now I knew it lived beyond her body.

Yes, my world had changed dramatically at 10:23 a.m. on August 8, 2002. But my soul was more deeply changed somewhere around twilight that night.

"There is a voice that doesn't use words. Listen."

— Rumi

Epilogue

"Ends are not bad things, they just mean that something else is about to begin. And there are many things that don't really end, anyway, they just begin again in a new way. Ends are not bad and many ends aren't really an ending; some things are never-ending."

— C. JoyBell C.

We left for Texas the next day. The migraine had cleared and the grief I had felt the day before settled into my bones, leaving me feeling heavy and weak. We traveled along our usual route and I thought about all the times we had made that trip with Keisha in the backseat. Every time her image appeared in my mind, the tears would march in an unobstructed deluge. I sat silently as the landscape zoomed by. This was a world now without Keisha in it.

The heat was oppressive and the drive seemed especially quiet.

My sadness bubbled to the surface at any provocation and I announced to my family that I did not want anyone to talk about her. I needed to let things settle within my own space. I enforced the rule in order to keep me safe from my grief.

But within a week, I was the one who broke my own rule. Memories of her place in our family paraded forward, and I became tired of controlling them and pushing the grief down, like a circus trainer coaxing the roaring animal back into his cage. Keisha's hilarious exploits seemed to trot into my thoughts, just as her little black body had done into my life 14 years ago.

As they surfaced I couldn't help but pull my family into the memories with me; the laughter began to bubble up and the sadness took a back seat. Soon Keisha seemed to be in the room with us: her sparkling eyes, her wagging tail, and her constant scavenging to sniff out a snack or an errant adventure. The laughter, the shared tears were balm to my pain, soothing and cool.

And I had tiny glimpses of feeling her presence, the way I had done during the twilight hours of August 8.

I thought of Jonathan and Duchess, of my mother and Blitzi. Of my father and Boots. Yes, Tennyson cast a tentative eye my way. Would I join the group who believed that to have loved and lost was better than to have never loved at all? Or would I be in the camp who vowed that this pain was too great a price to pay? Keisha had taught me that broken hearts could heal. And that they could be broken again. She had done both for me.

We returned home, to our new, cold, tile floor, and began a new chapter of life. Little did I know that around that time a large and furry being was making his way to pen #11 at the Carlsbad Animal Shelter, just a few miles from our house. He, too, had suffered a heavy loss and carried the pain with him to his new beginning

When the student is ready for more lessons, the Master arrives.

Acknowledgements

I vividly remember sitting in the journalism lab at the University of Texas in the spring of 1985. I was typing away at the computer terminal, desperately trying to finish my latest assignment. As I tapped out the current news story, I knew in that moment that I wanted to write a book someday. I was twenty-one years old, thought I knew a lot about life, and accepted this realization with the grace of youth.

I shared my excitement of that goal with my father one day who enthusiastically said, "Great! What's it going to be about?"

Ah, there was the rub. I didn't have a story.

Throughout the years I searched desperately for my story. A mystery? A comedy? A WWII spy novel? But nothing tangible ever showed up. I joined the corporate world and immersed myself in a career. "How's that book coming?" my father would ask. I would shake my head and answer, "I don't have the story yet, Dad." But I could still feel it. Yes, it was there. But I couldn't see it.

The years flew by: I became a wife, a mother and changed careers. "What about the book?" my dad questioned, reminding me of that dream now years in the past.

I had not yet realized I was living it.

It would be a while before Keisha said to me in the unspoken, unwritten language she and I shared, "I just gave you a story. Now write it." As vibrant and strong a character as Keisha was, she was no match for the self-doubts and myriad reasons explaining away why I couldn't write the book. I would meet an inspirational friend and counselor, Guylaine Vallee, whose talents included reading the meandering, branching lines on my hand and translated them into a directive: write! But my fears were strong even in the face of such direct and loving encouragement.

And yet it unfolded in its own perfect way. I began writing. And stopped. And wrote some more. And stopped again. It was in fits and starts that those years with Keisha emerged onto the page. Tired of the doubts and qualms while continually moving the book to my most current "To-Do" list, I signed up for a writing retreat and my book finally moved from within me onto the page and into the world.

I am deeply grateful for those who were participants in this story. You each walked beside me, along my path, and played vital roles in my life. I want to extend a heartfelt thanks to each person who lent their talents and their support to me as this book took its physical form. I am forever in debt to two soulmates in particular: Sharon CassanoLochman and Ernestine Colombo. You both saved me at the eleventh hour-- with an emergency Zoom meeting across three time zones and a big dose of unconditional love. It doesn't get better than that!

Most especially I want to thank my father, who passed away just a short time before this book was published. Dad, you were always my greatest champion in life and the best father anyone could wish for. I know you and Keisha are watching over me.

I wish someone had told me, as I sat in the journalism lab all those years ago, "Don't worry, Lily. Your story will come. You have no idea what's in store for you. Be patient. Observe. You can never know how things will unfold and bloom."

But maybe uncertainty *is* one of the beautiful parts of the journey.

Keisha and the author
North Carolina 1996

About the Author

Lily Tanzer is a native Texan, born and raised in Austin. Always intrigued by human behavior, she earned a degree in Psychology from the University of Texas in 1985. At the age of twenty six, she welcomed a renegade dog into her life who further extended her studies in behavior-- human and canine. Tanzer currently lives in southern California with her husband and two dogs.

www.ingramcontent.com/pod-product-compliance
Lightning Source LLC
Chambersburg PA
CBHW030509080526
44586CB00011B/128